Meditation
color by numbers

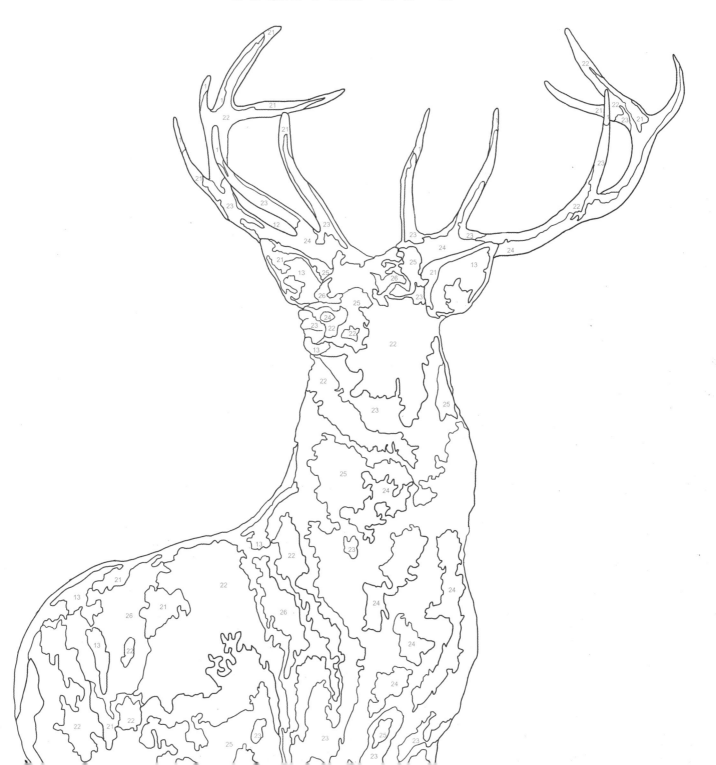

Meditation
color by numbers

Arpad Olbey

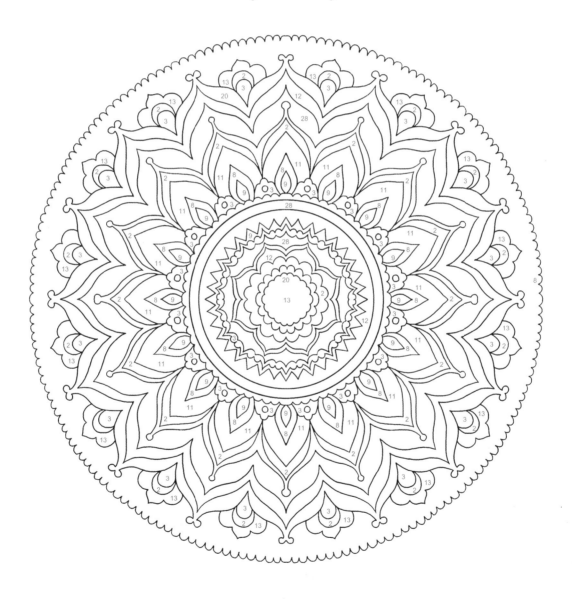

SIRIUS

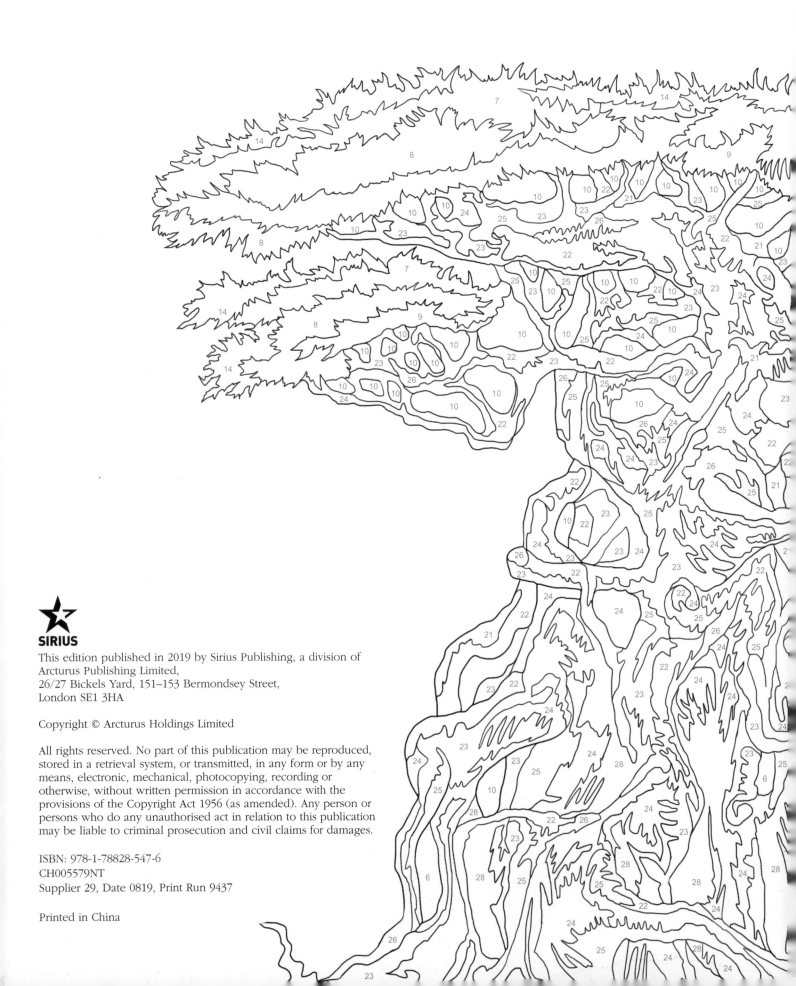

SIRIUS

This edition published in 2019 by Sirius Publishing, a division of
Arcturus Publishing Limited,
26/27 Bickels Yard, 151–153 Bermondsey Street,
London SE1 3HA

ISBN: 978-1-78828-547-6
CH005579NT
Supplier 29, Date 0819, Print Run 9437

Printed in China

INTRODUCTION

Taking time to reflect on our lives and the wonderful planet we live on is essential to our well-being. Sometimes in the hustle and bustle of modern life it can be hard to slow down and to escape thoughts of deadlines, money, and other pressures. Meditation is about setting aside those everyday concerns, taking the time to calm your thoughts and to experience the present moment. This collection of color-by-number images takes meditation as its theme, showing poses from the ancient practice of yoga and other relaxing, focused activities such as painting, fishing, and hiking. There are images celebrating the beauty of the natural world, from calming sunsets and gardens to majestic waterfalls and mountains. You will also find numerous patterns for coloring, including the circular mandala patterns that are used to represent the universe in Hindu and Buddhist symbolism.

All the images are numbered and the numbers match the color key to be found on the back cover flap. Match your pencils as closely as possible to the colors in the key—you can even label the pencils with numbers to make things easier. If there is no number that means the space should be left white or colored with a white pencil.

With color-by-number images you don't need to worry about getting a drawing right or even choosing which colors to use. This leaves you free to focus on the process of coloring and to enjoy the relaxation it can bring.

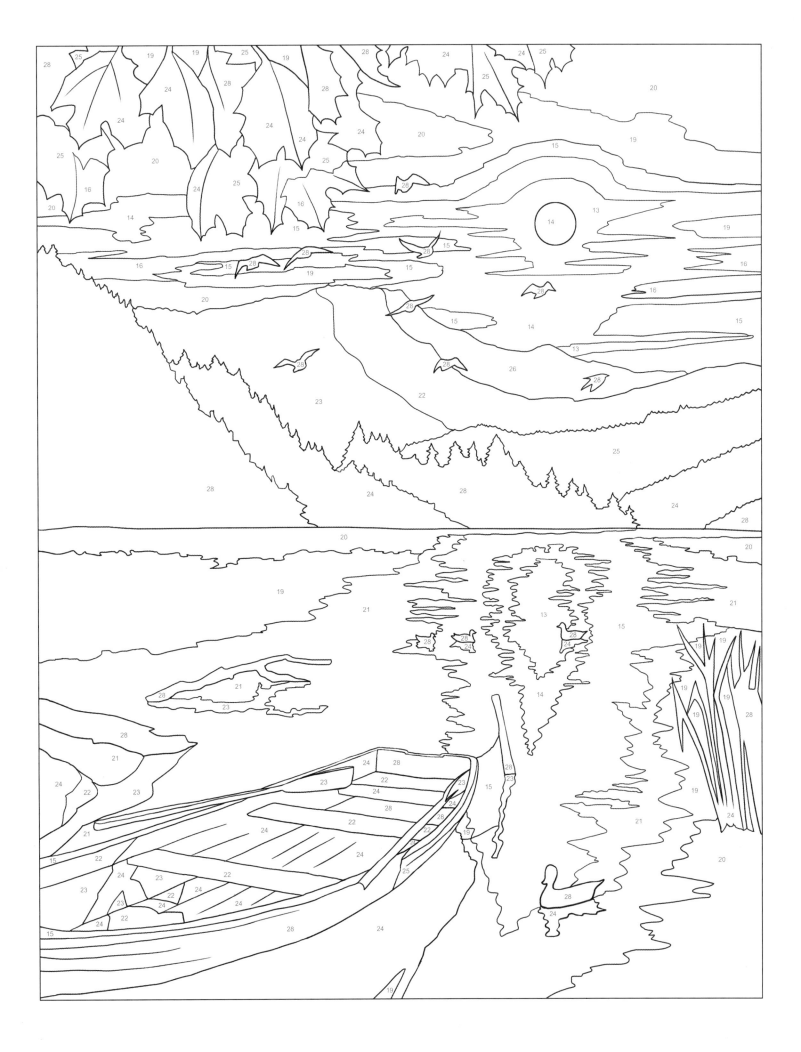

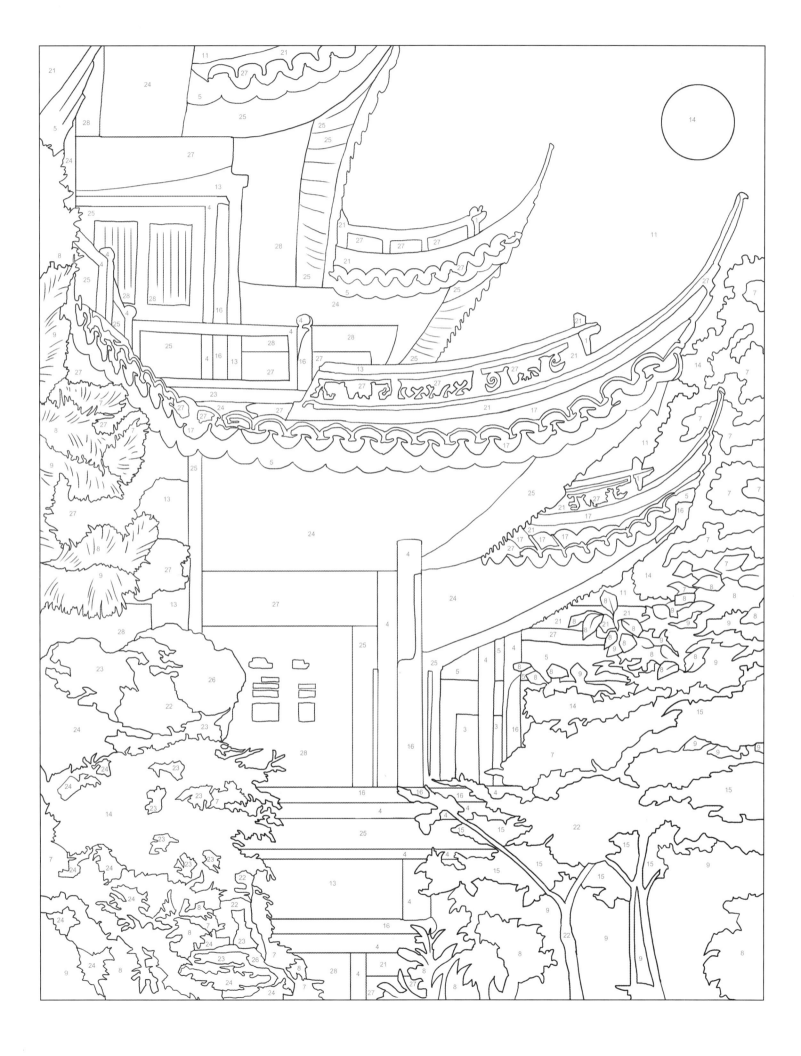

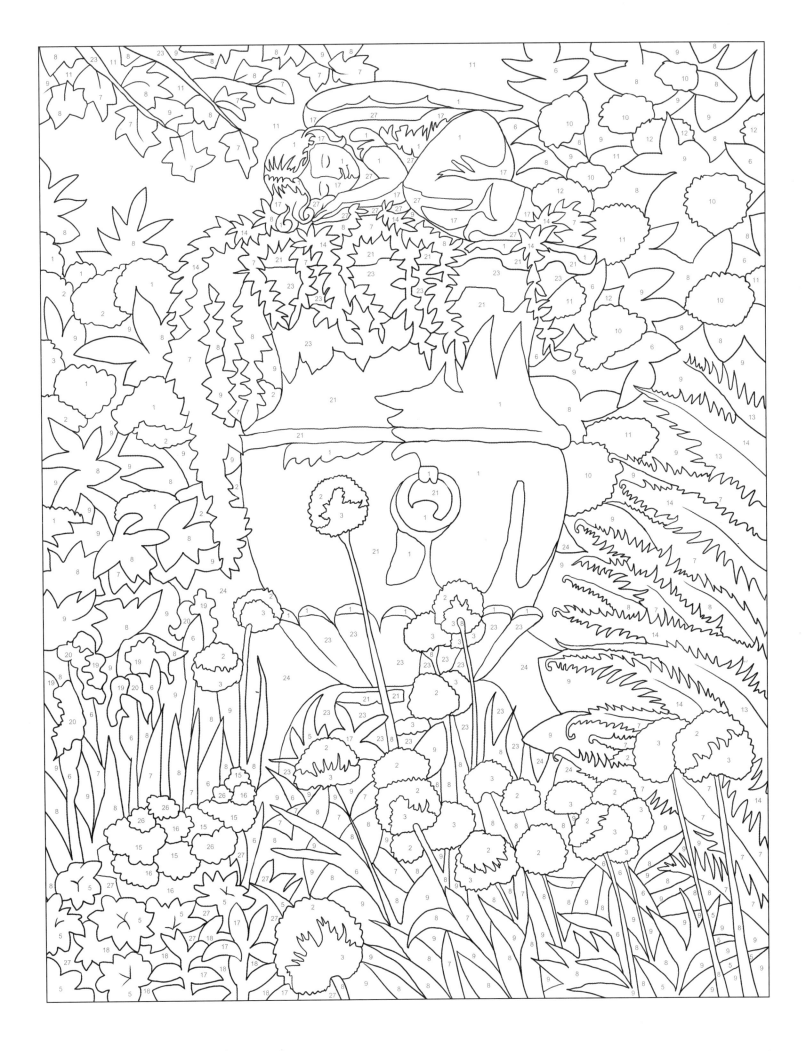

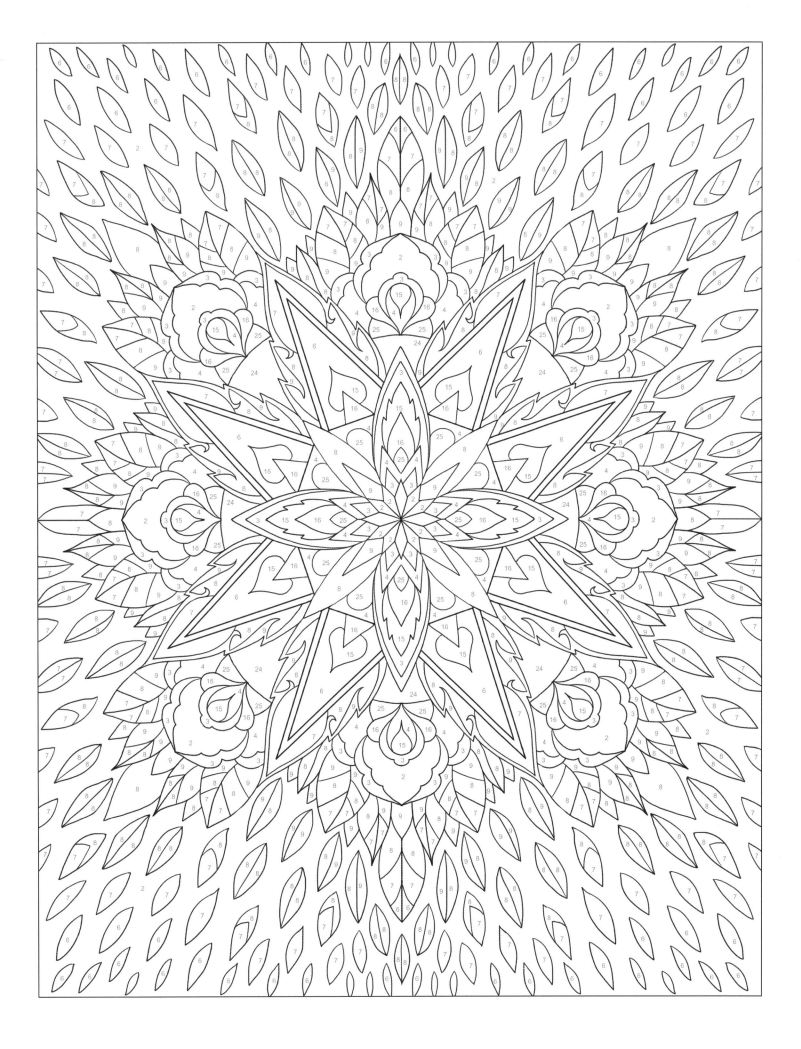

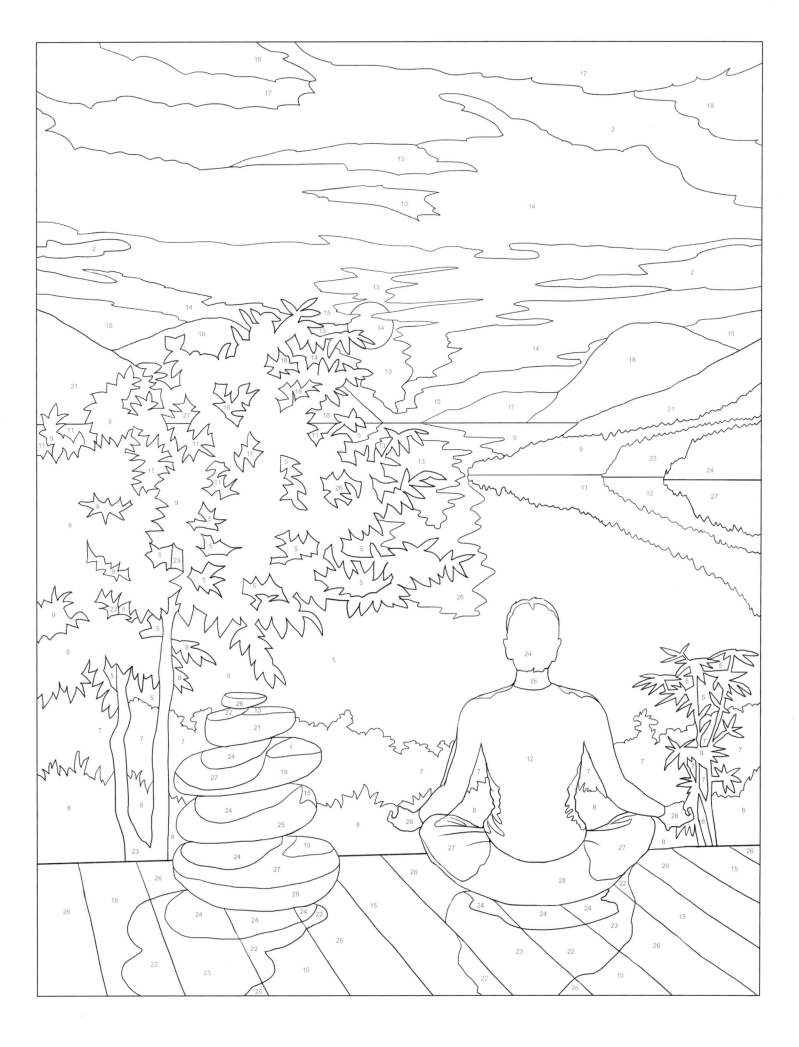

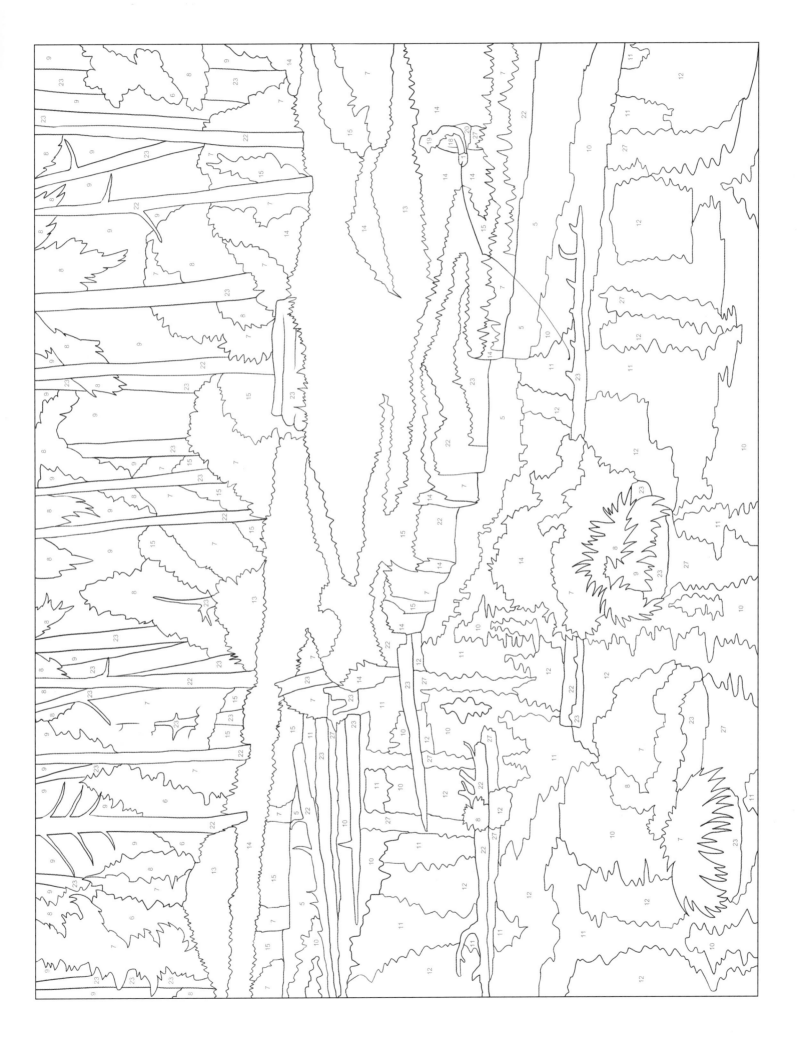

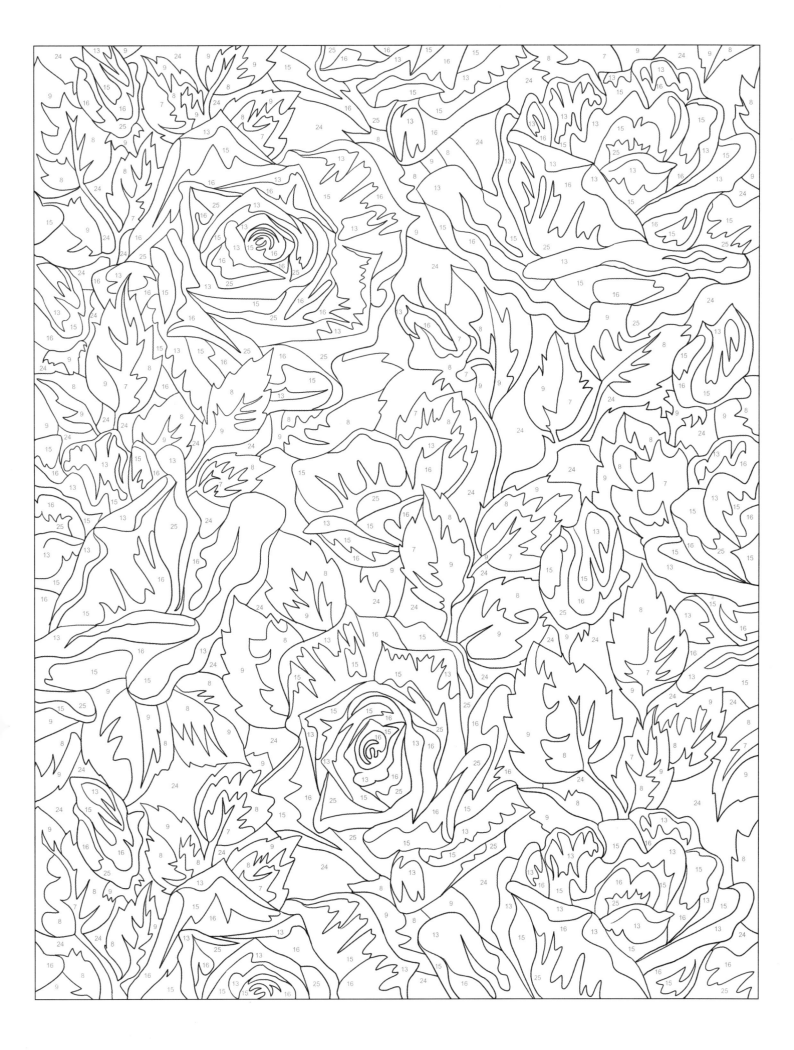

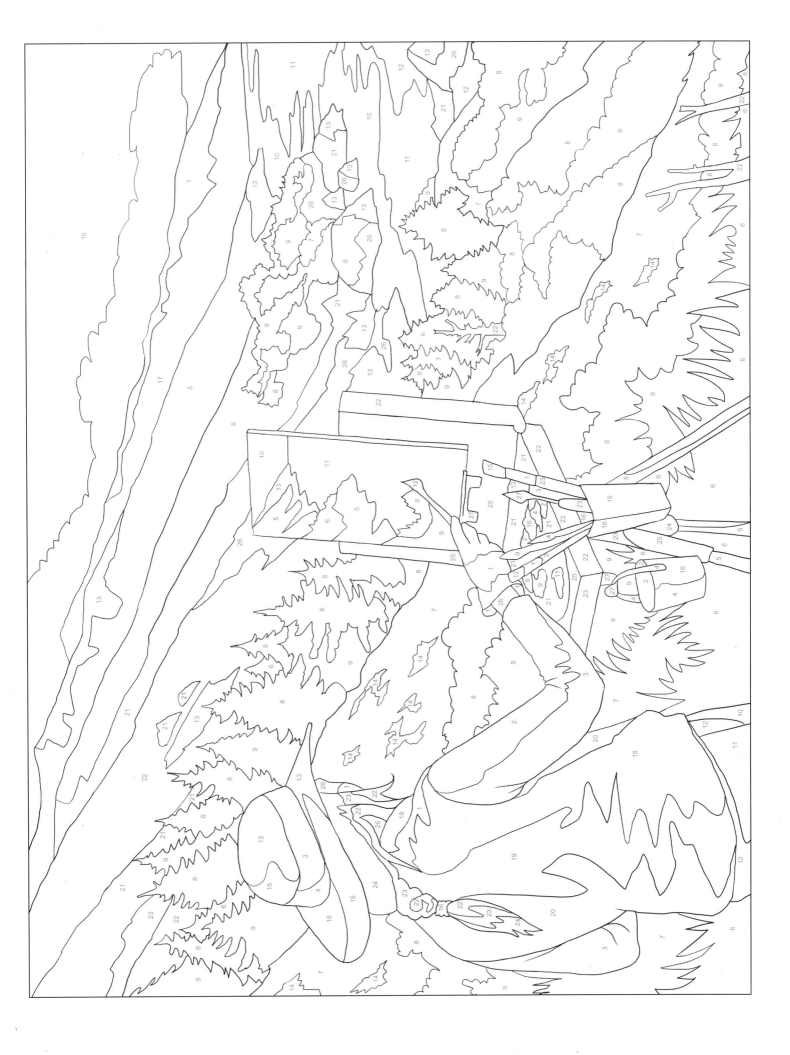

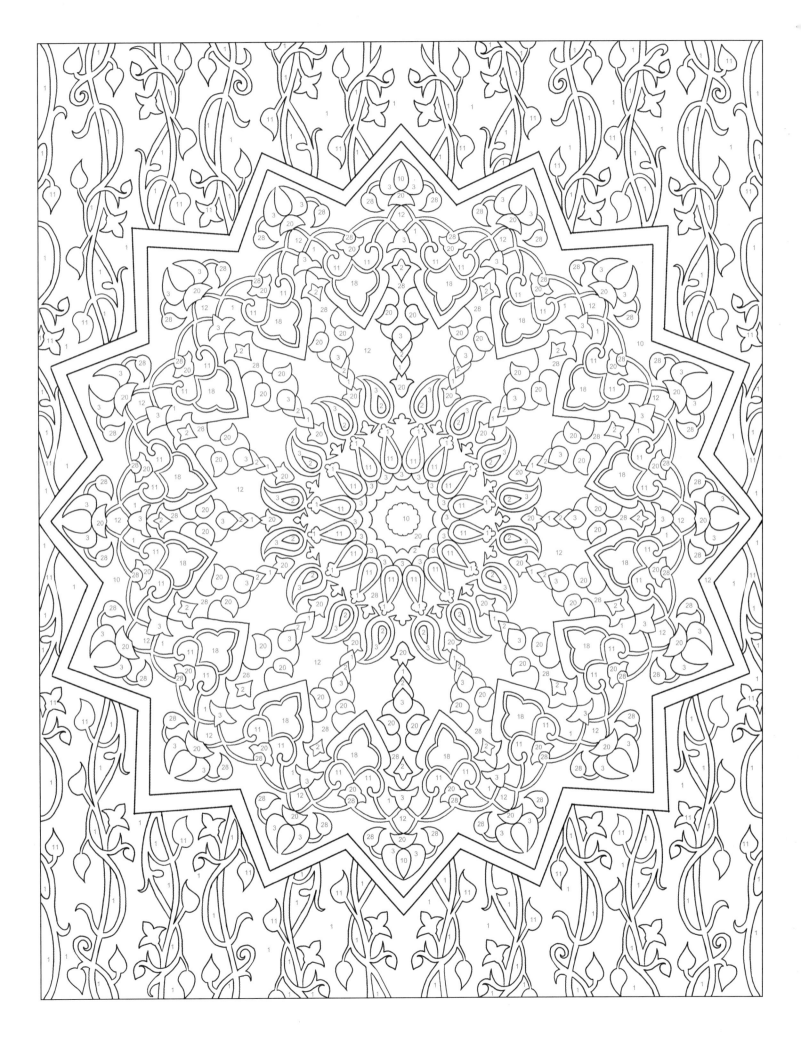

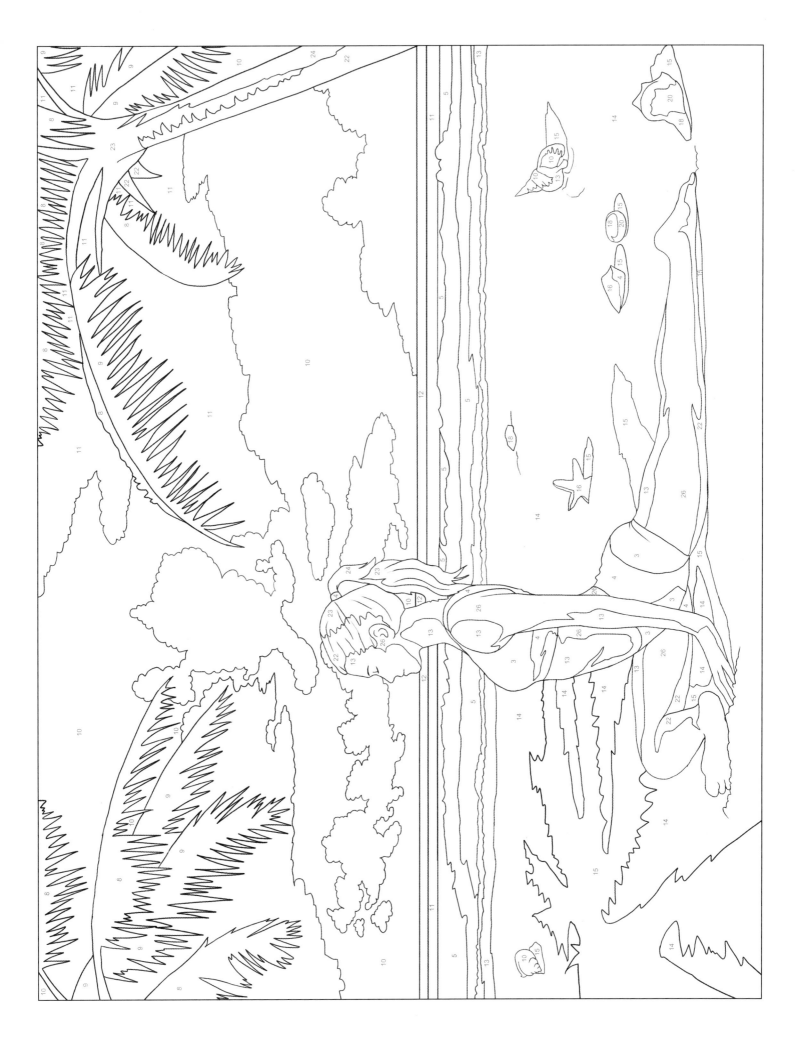

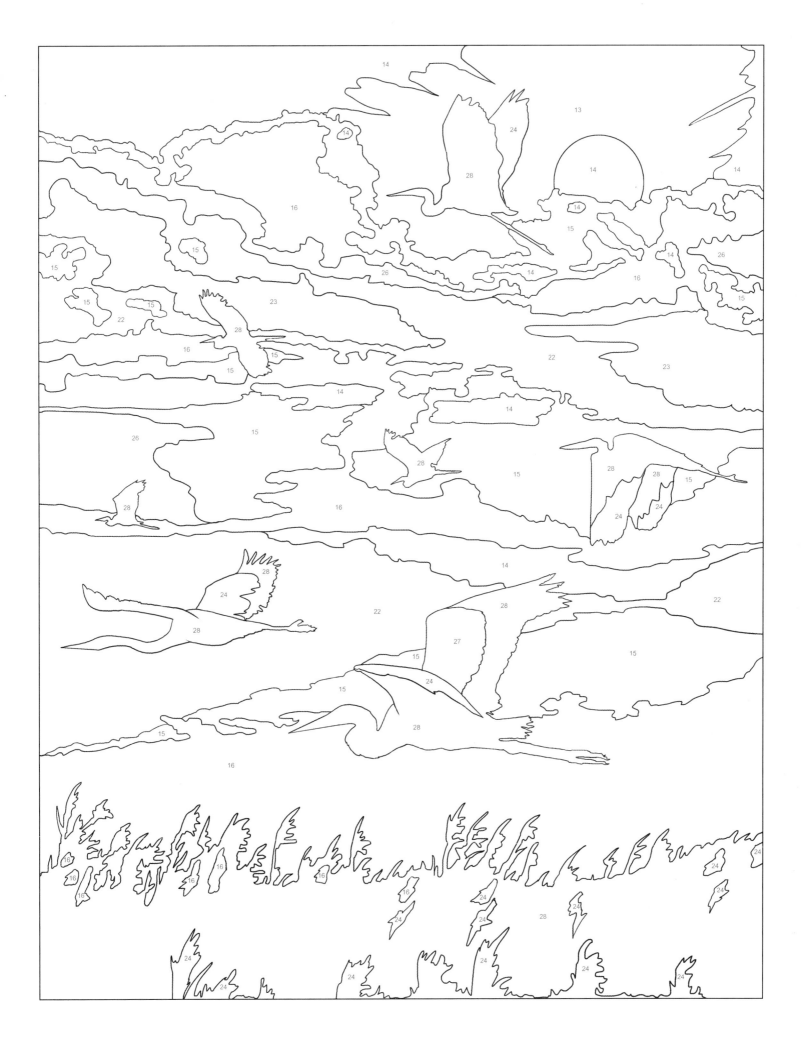

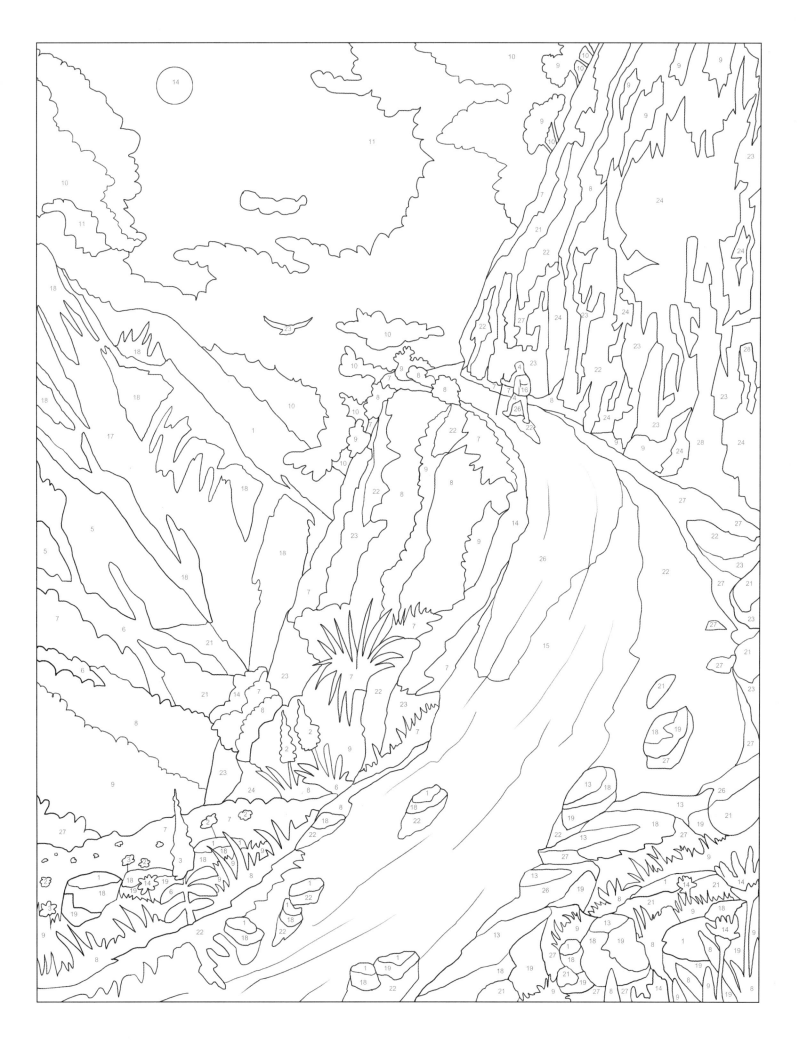

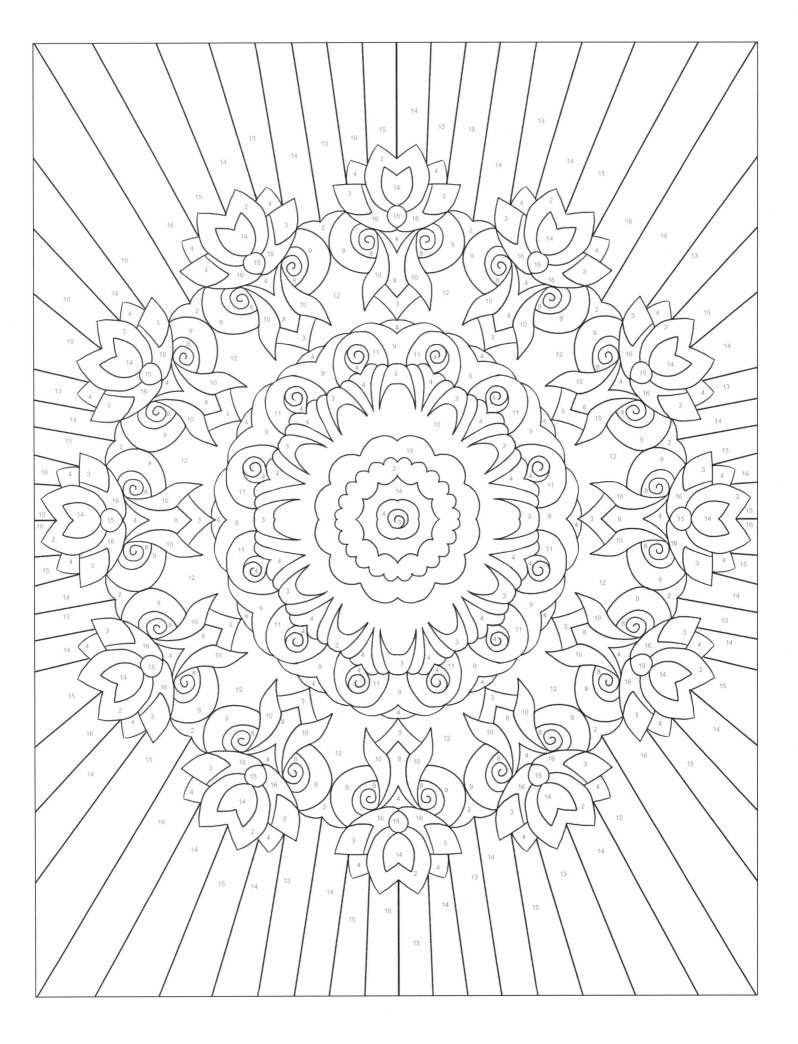

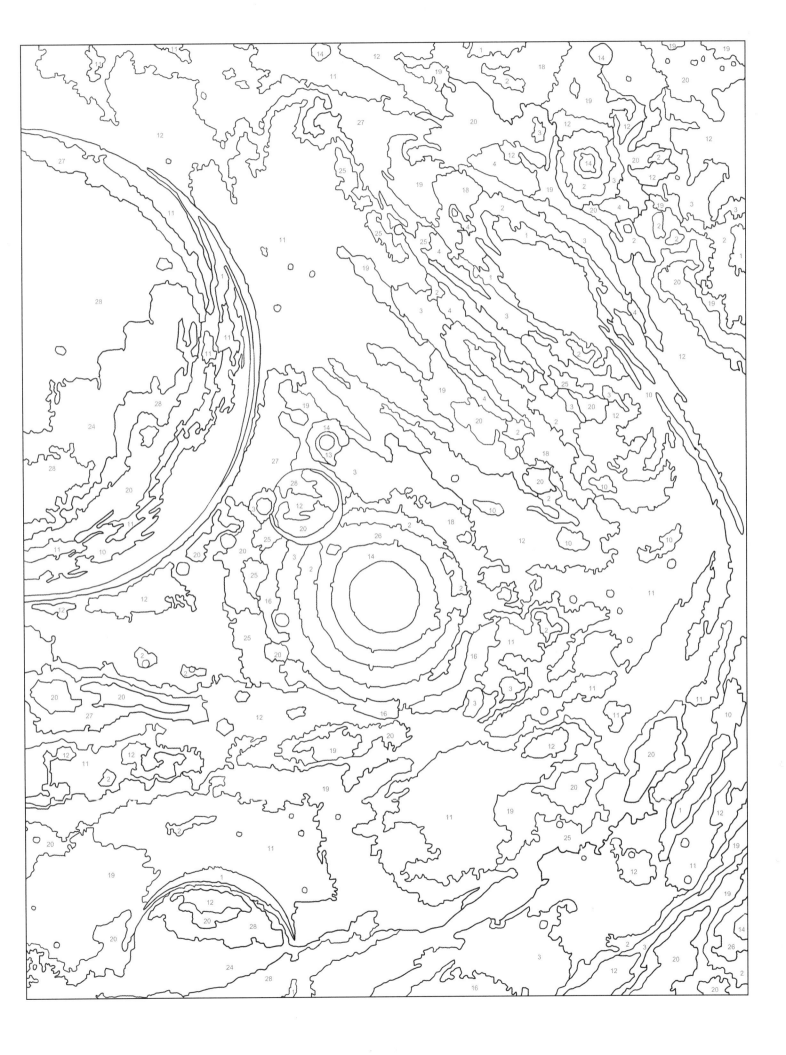

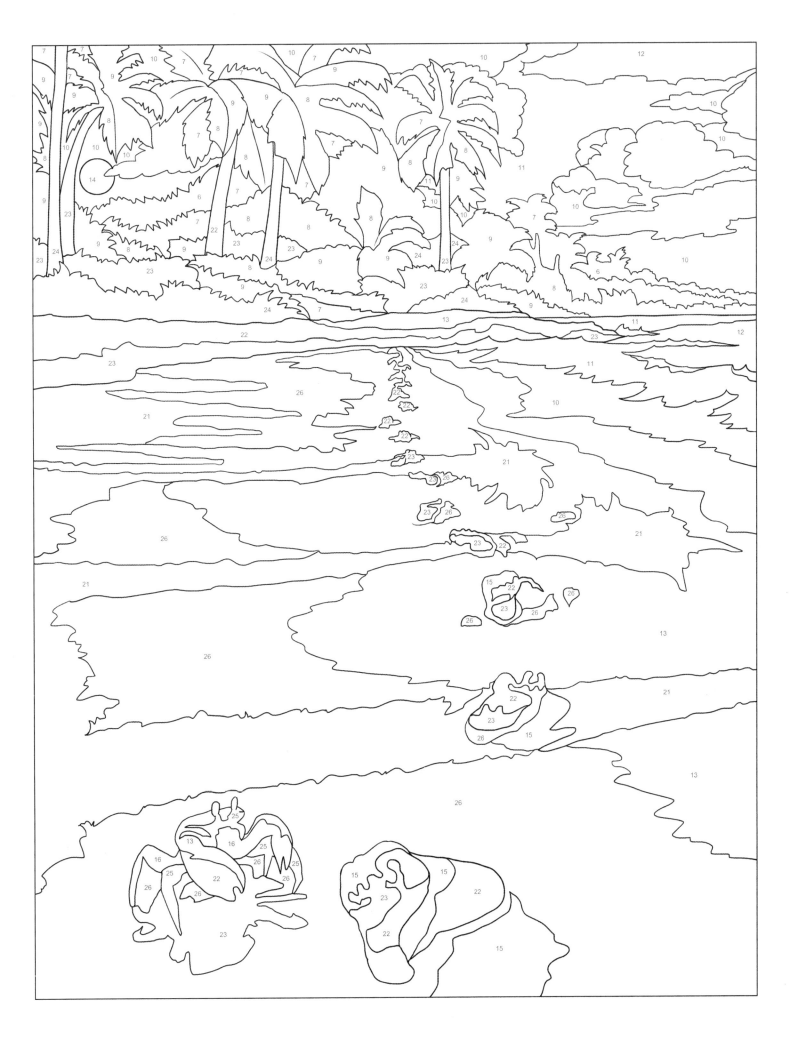

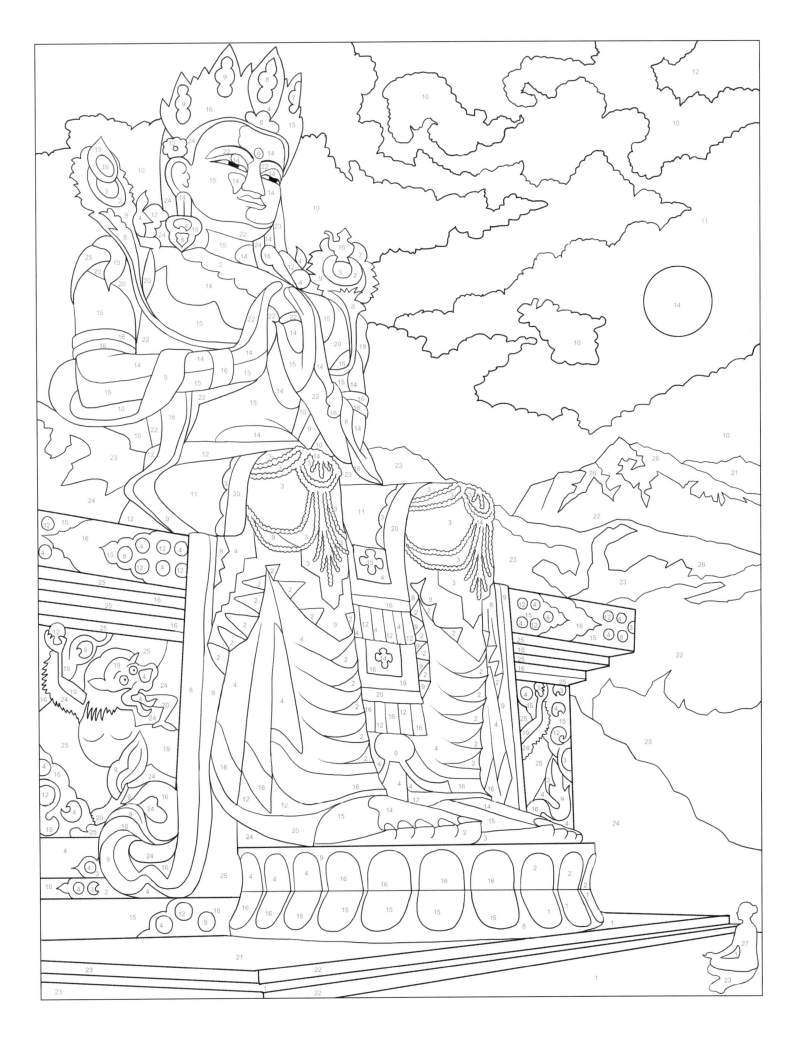

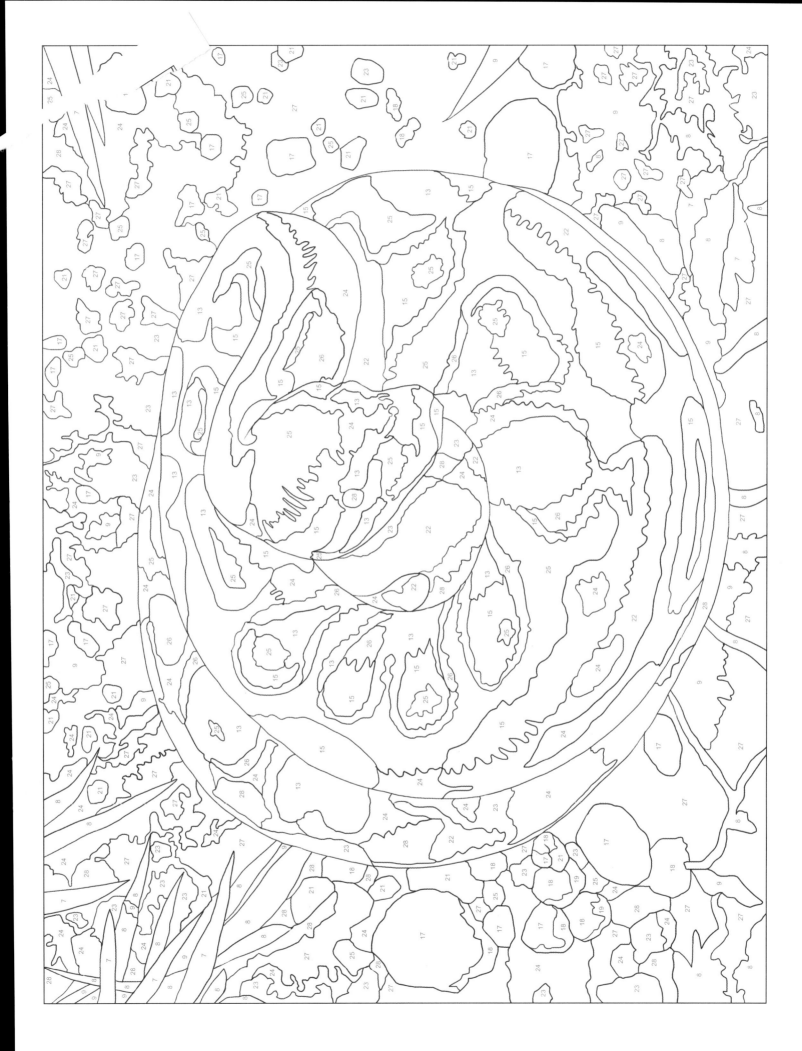

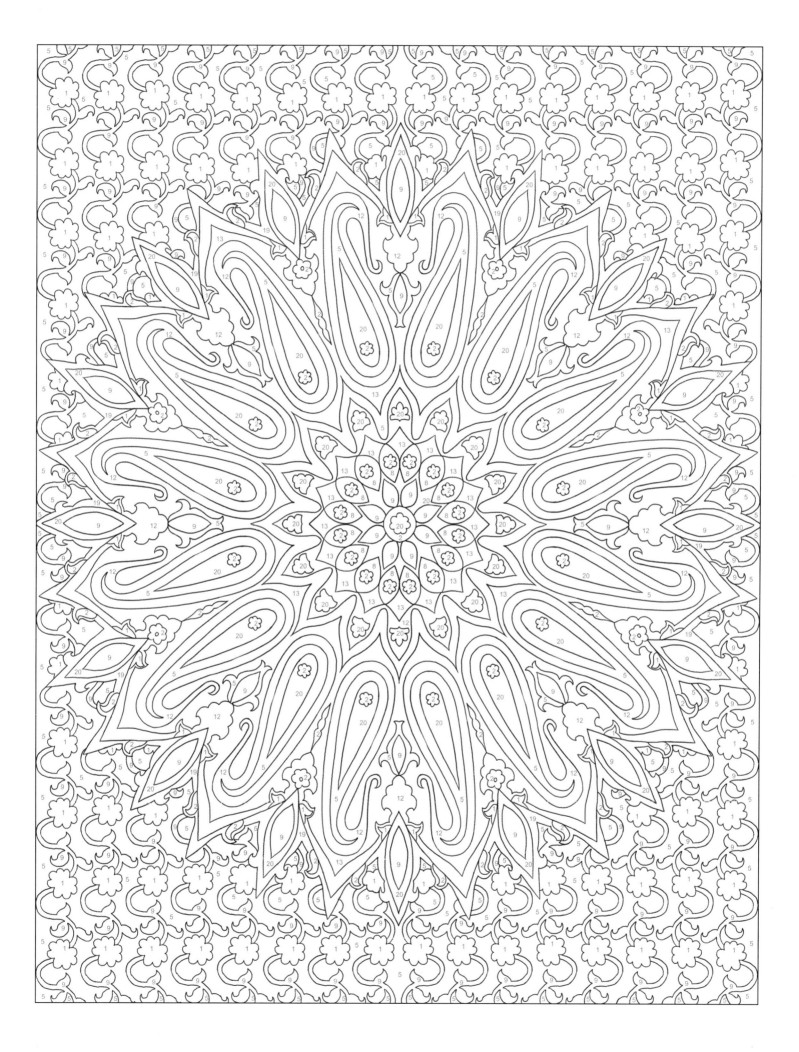

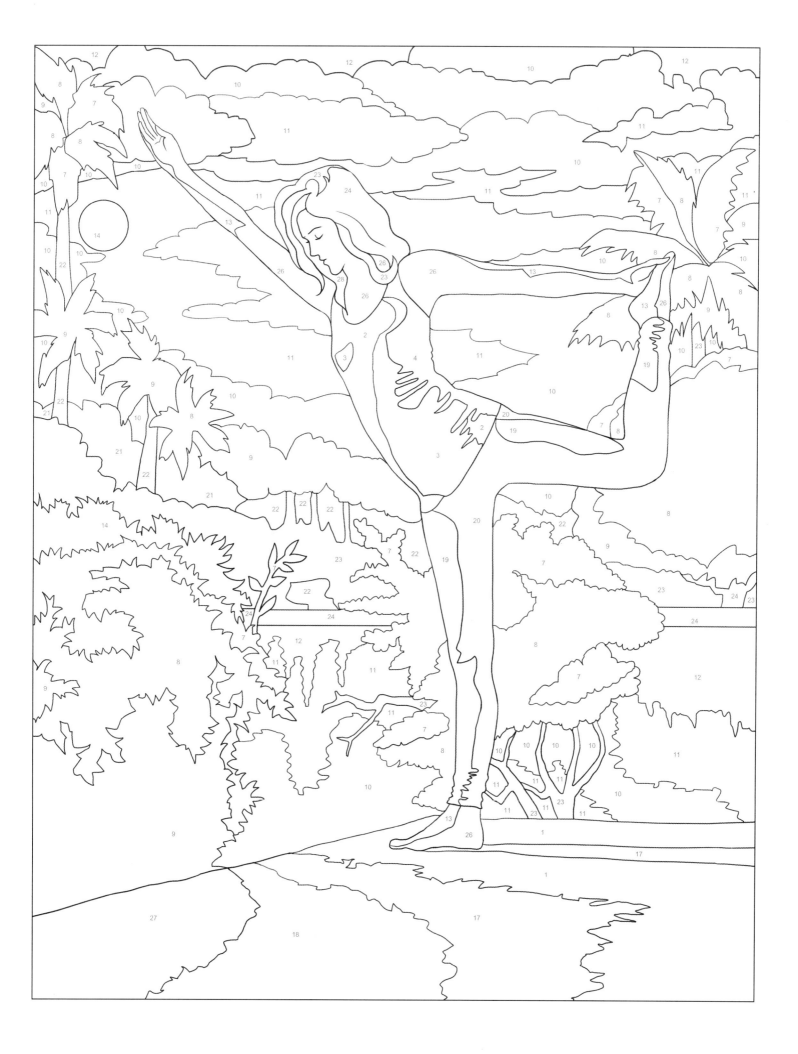

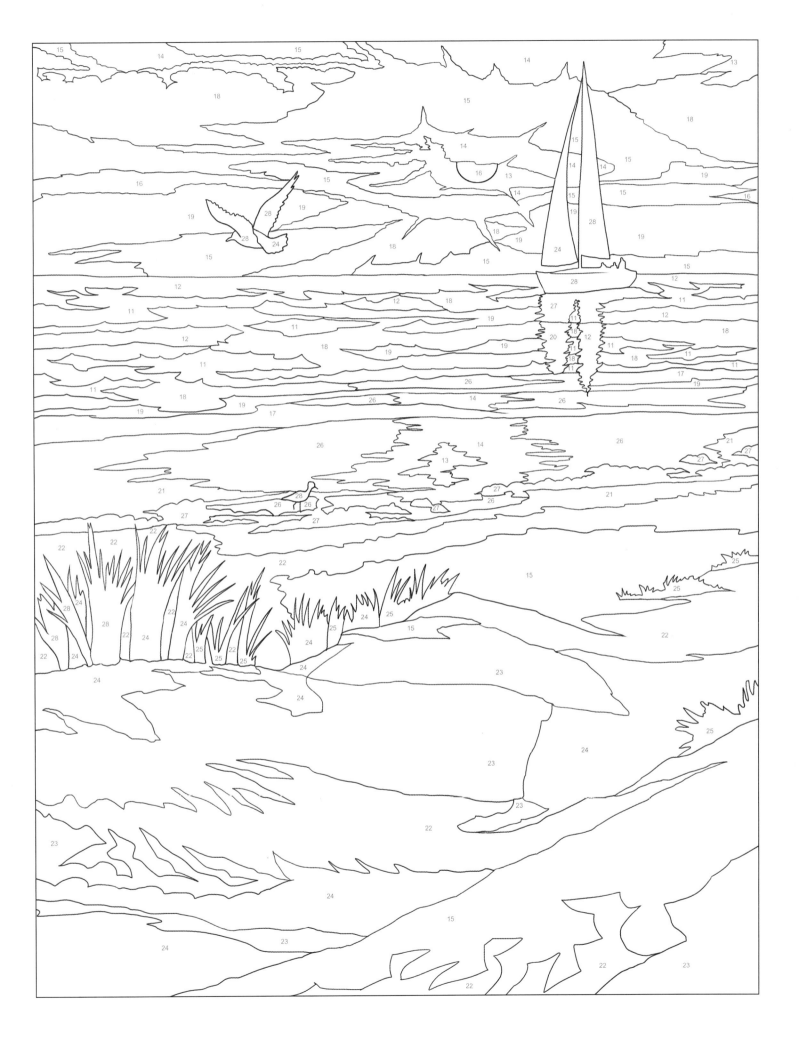

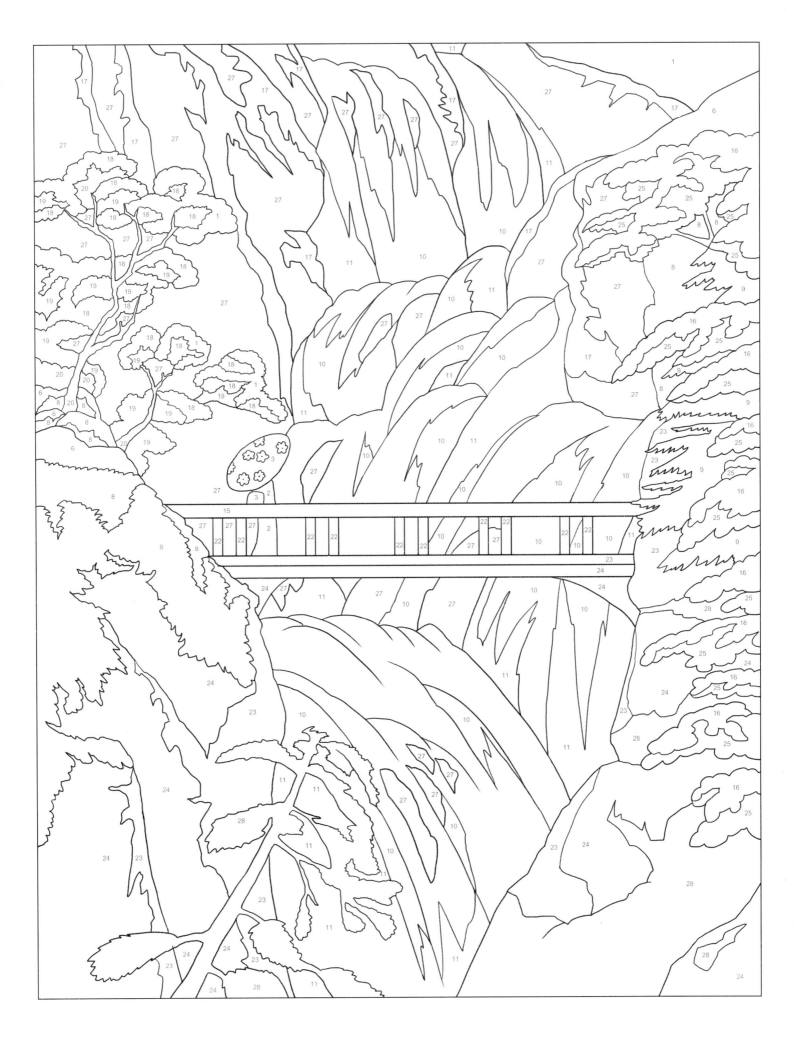

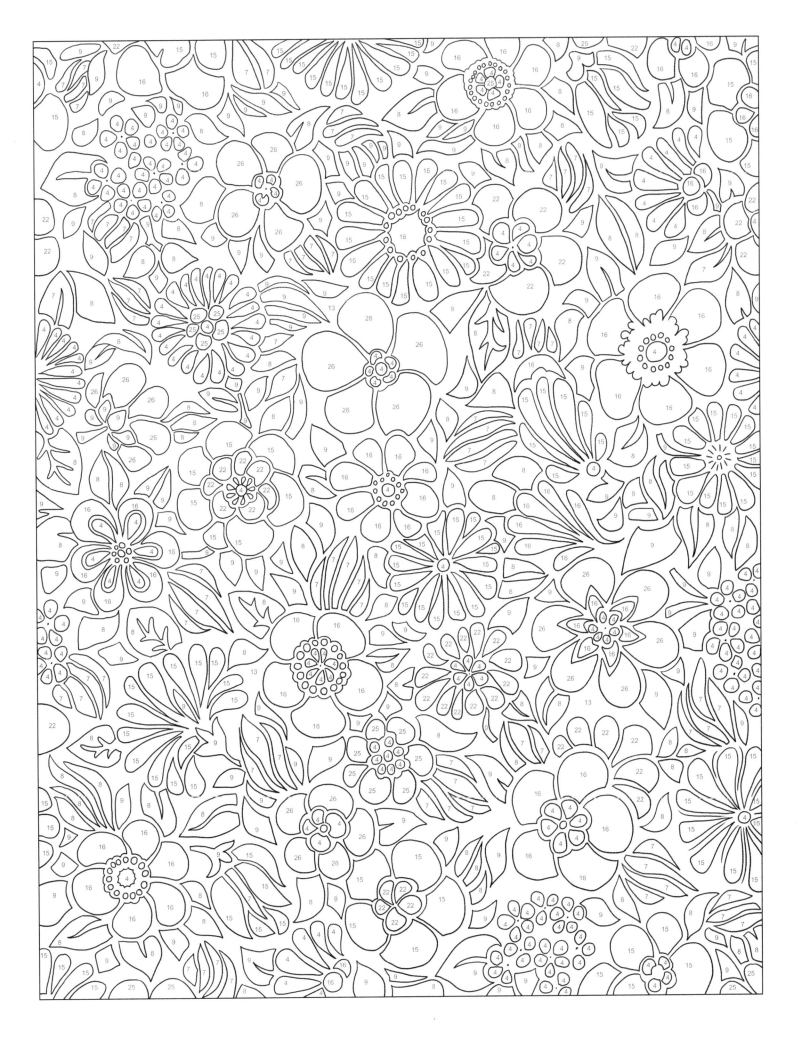

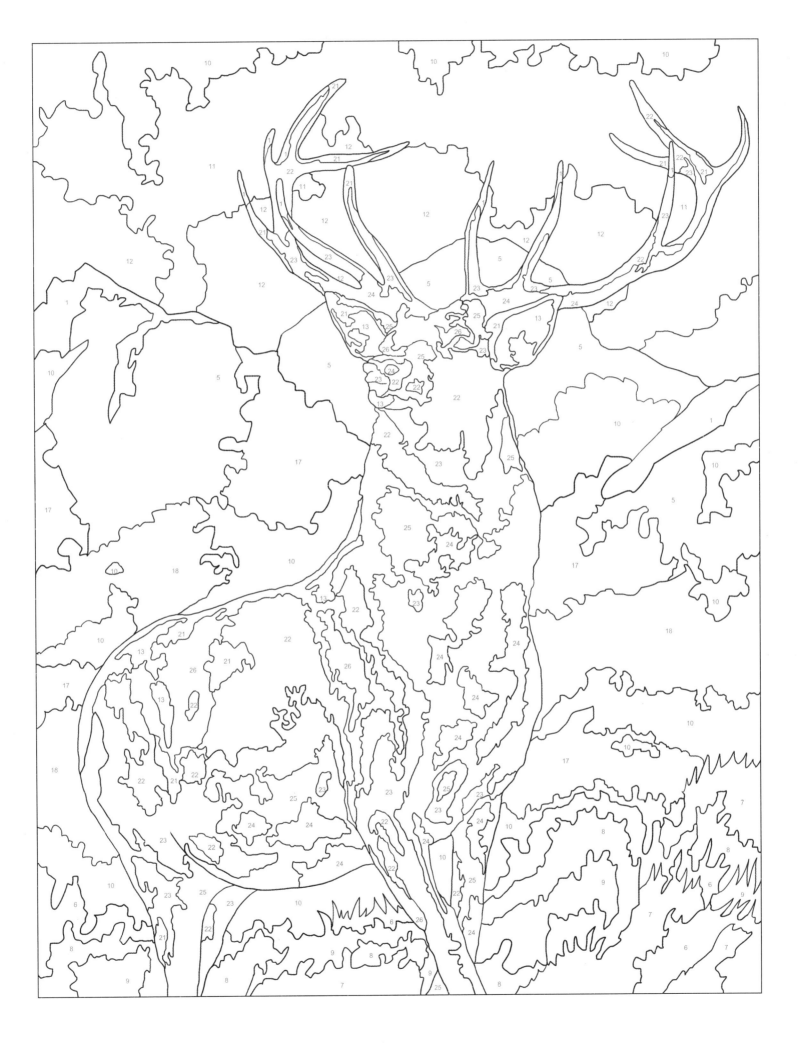

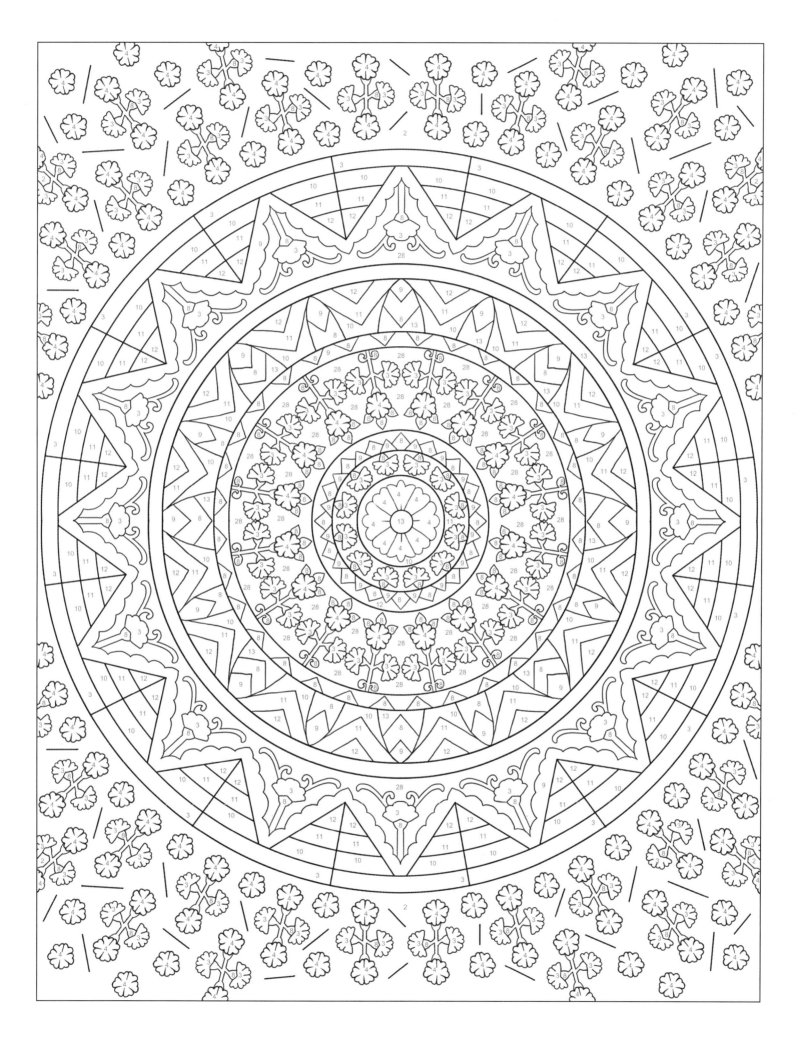

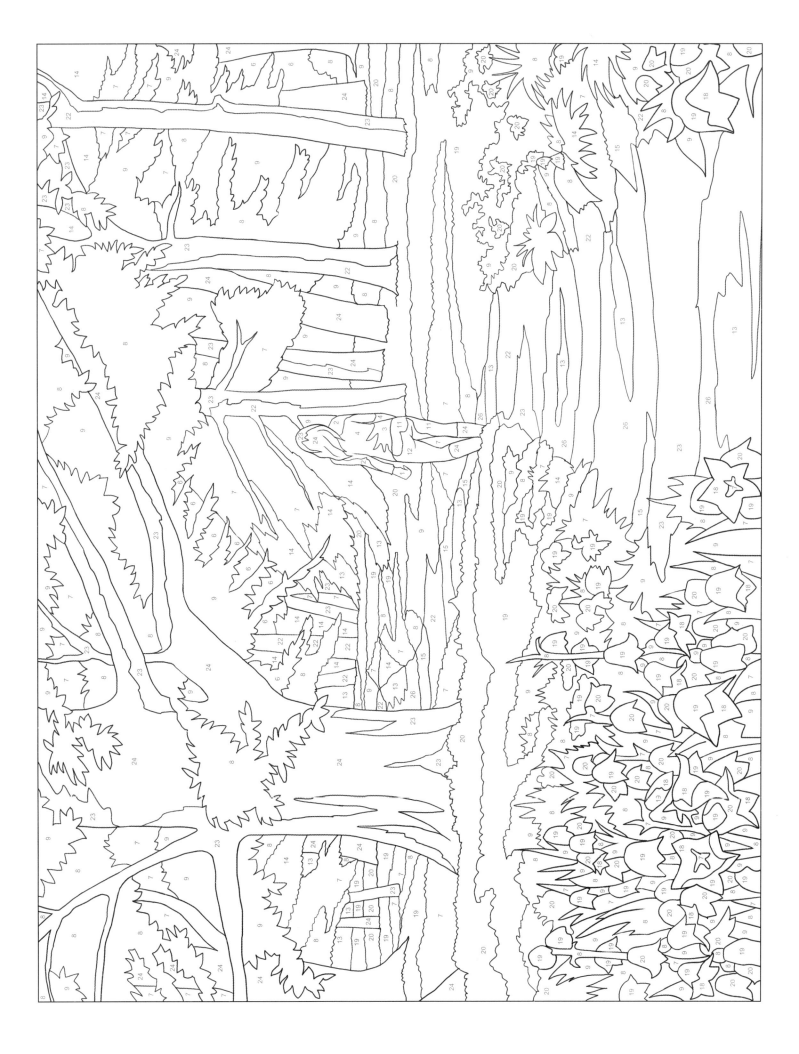

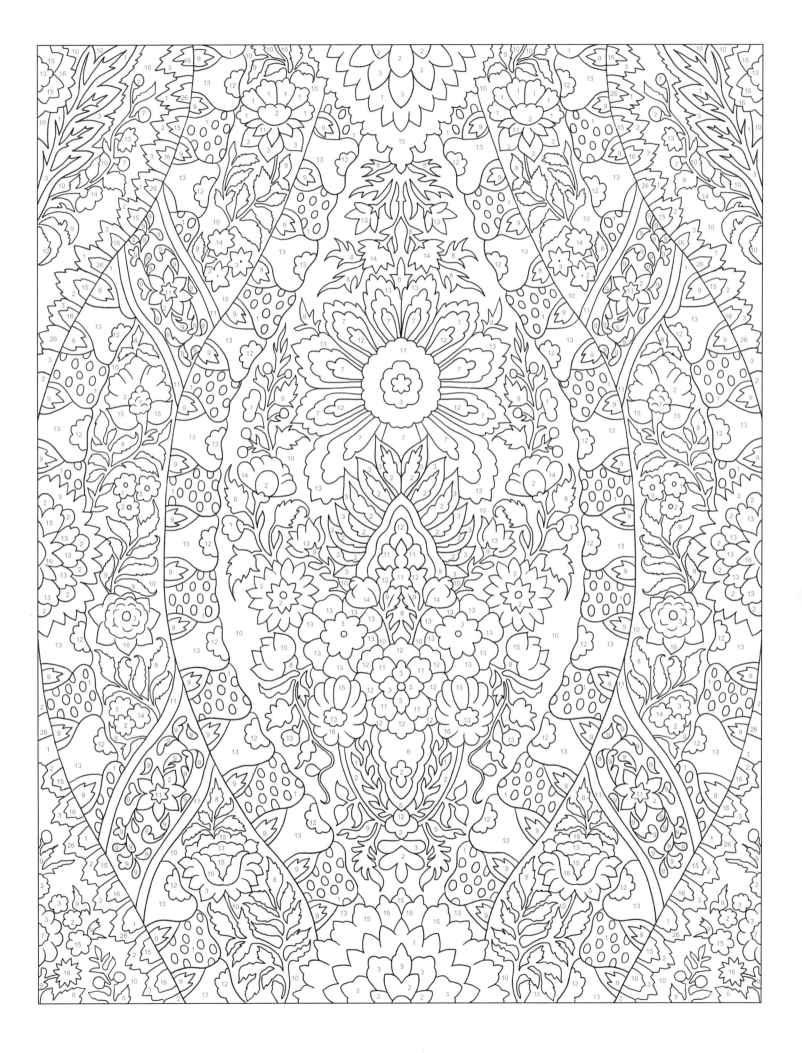

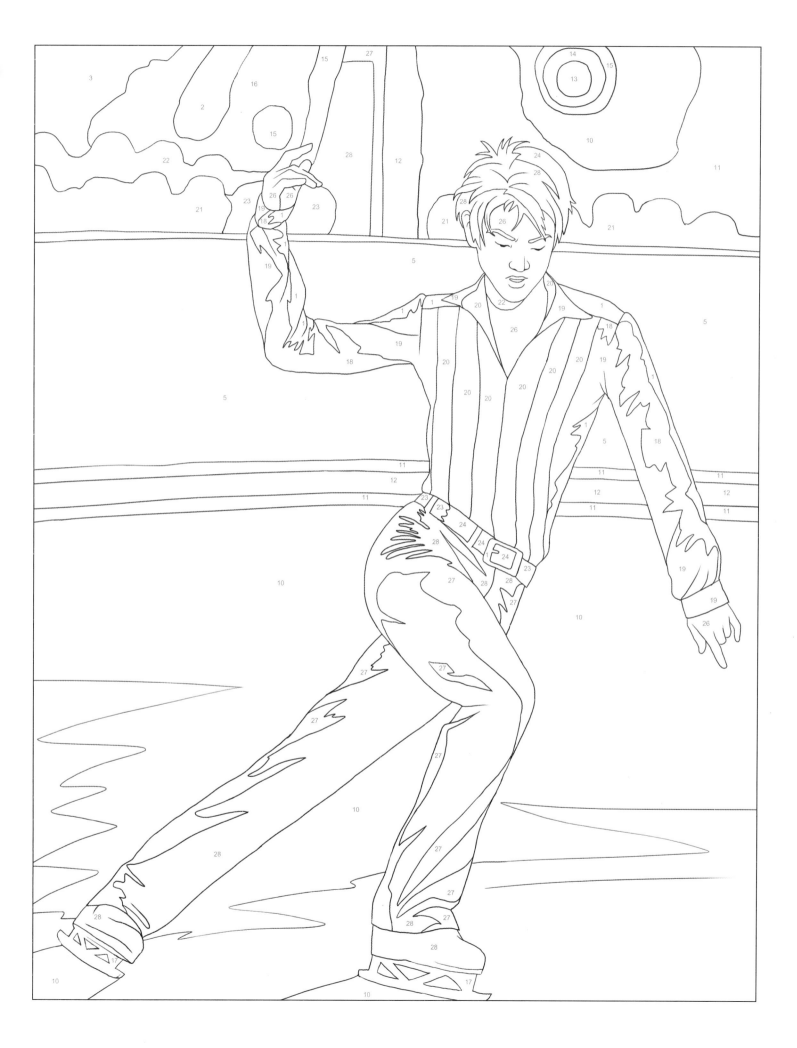

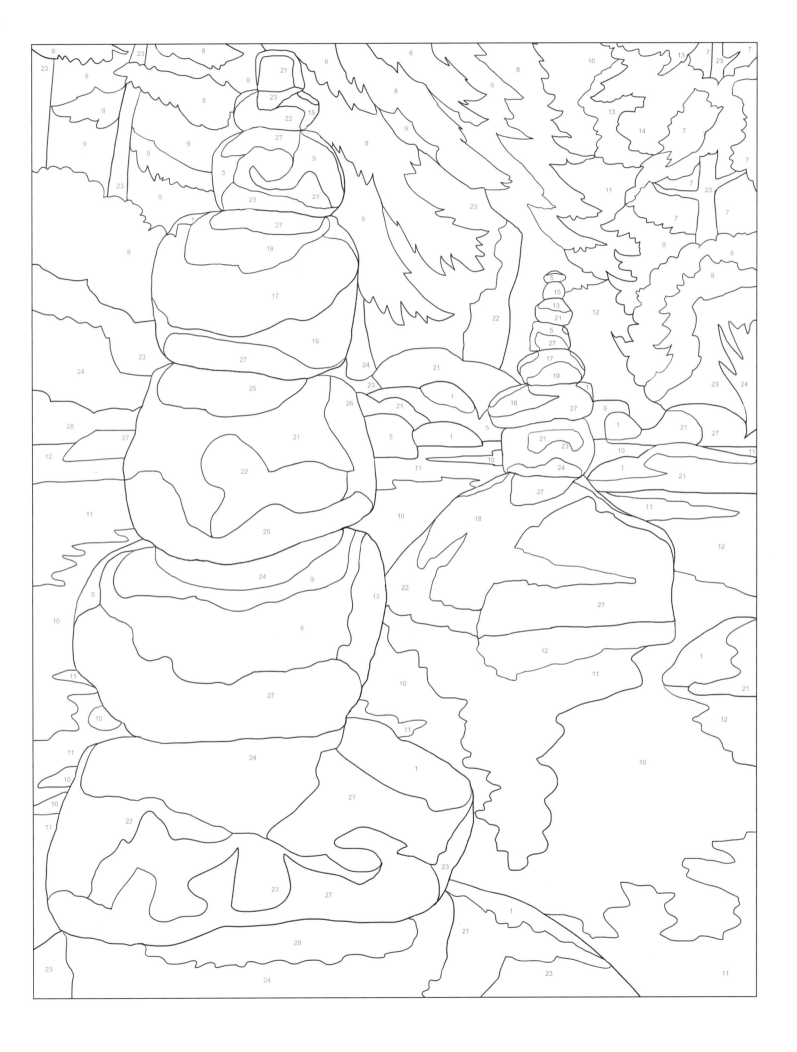

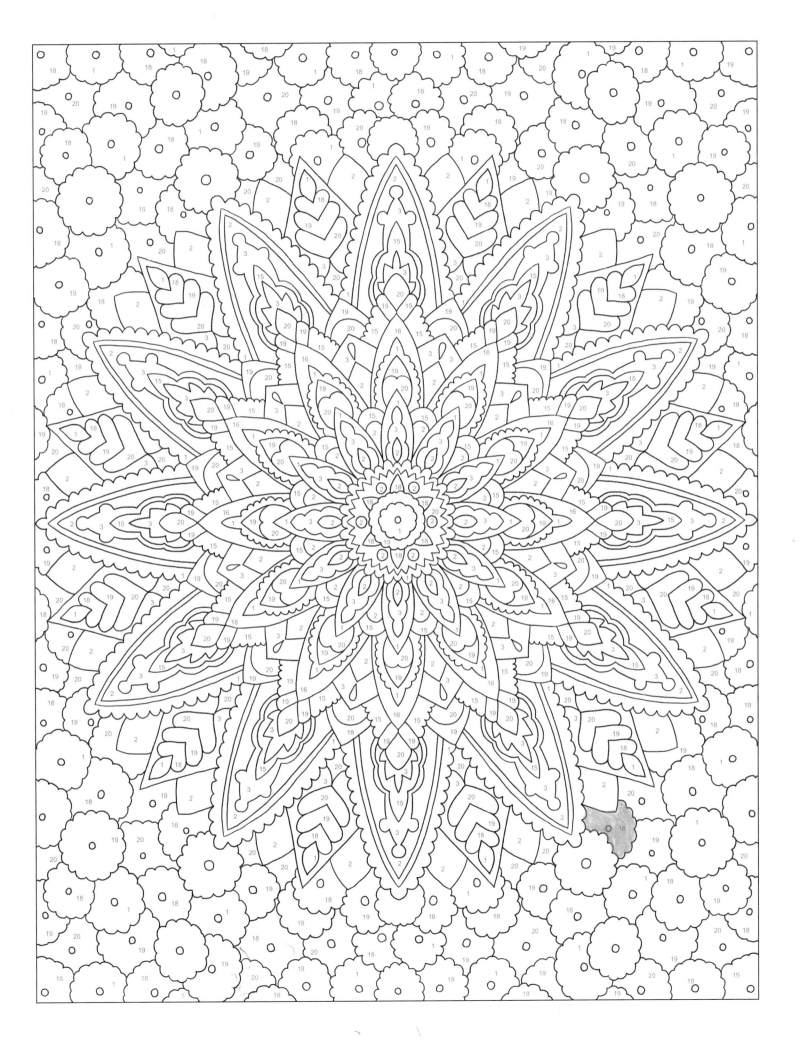

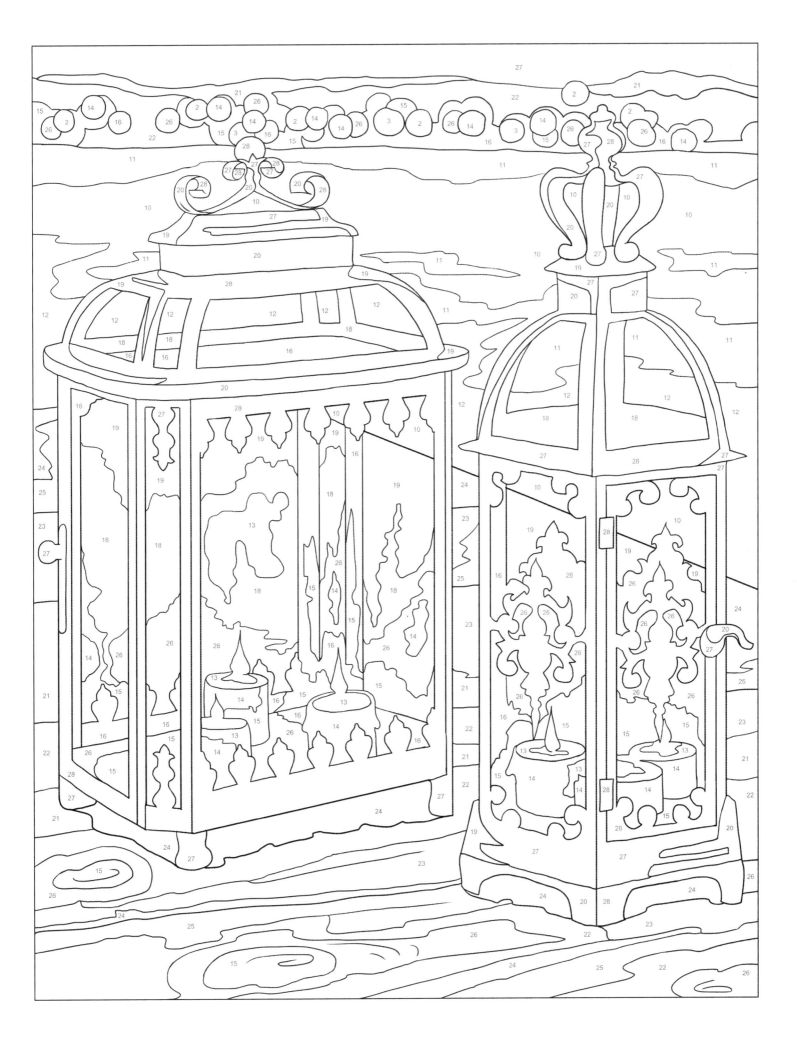

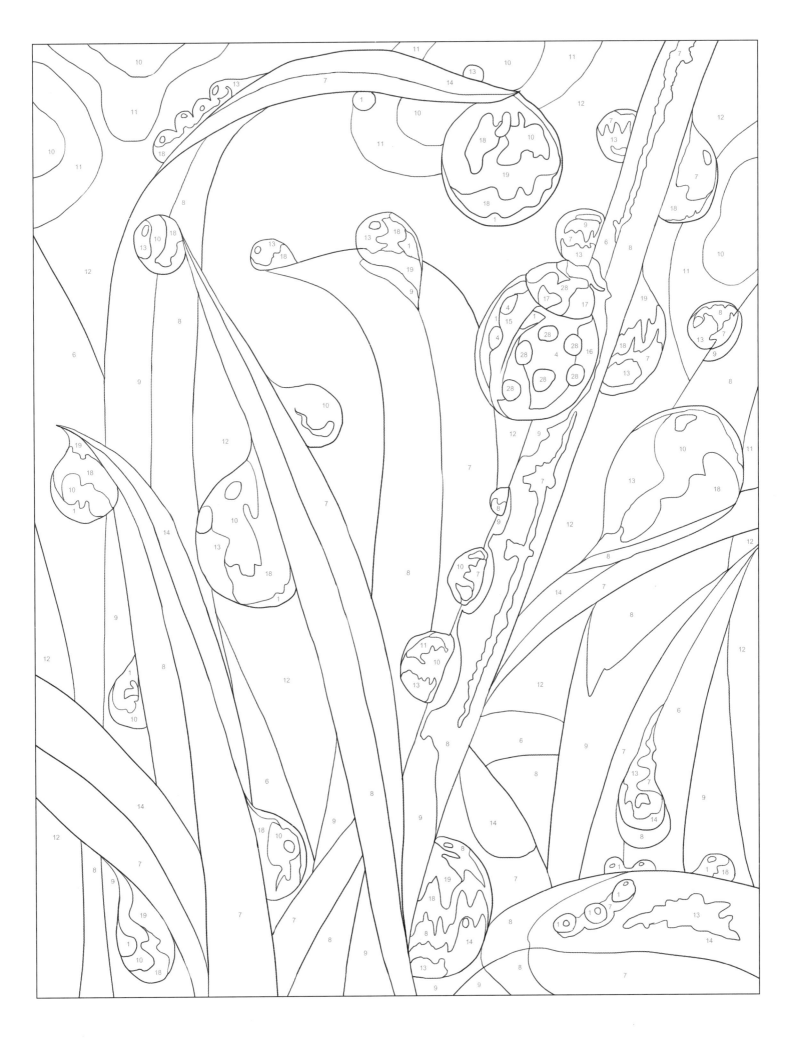

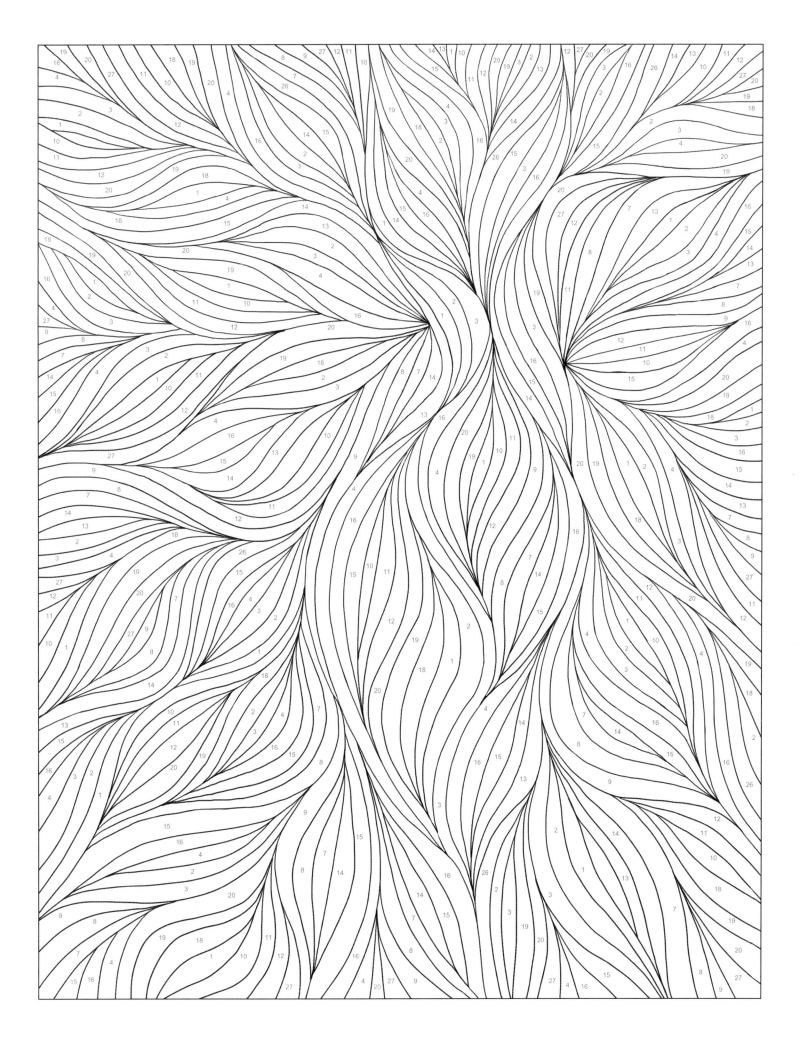

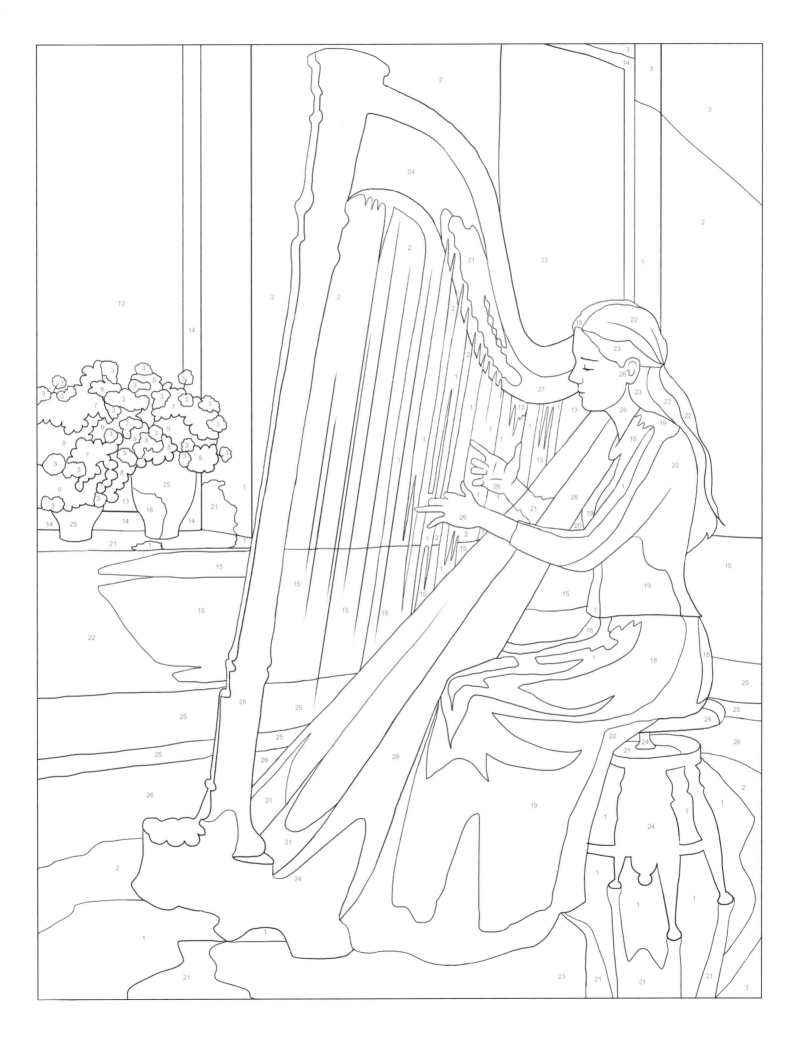

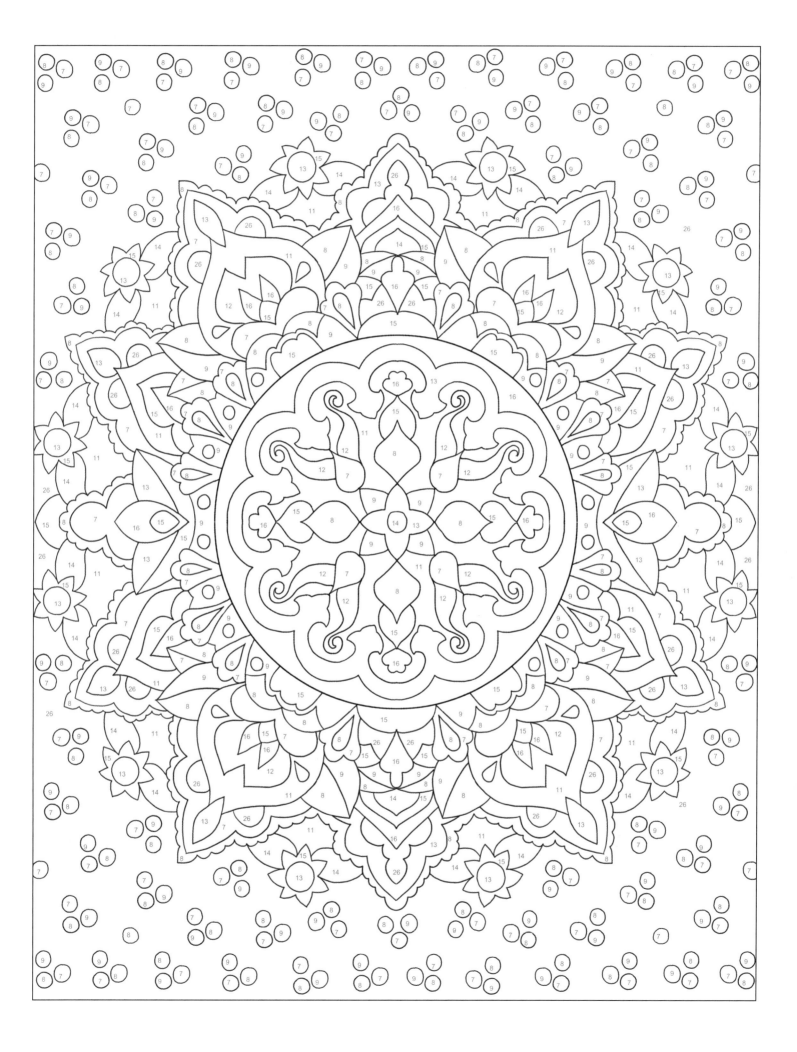

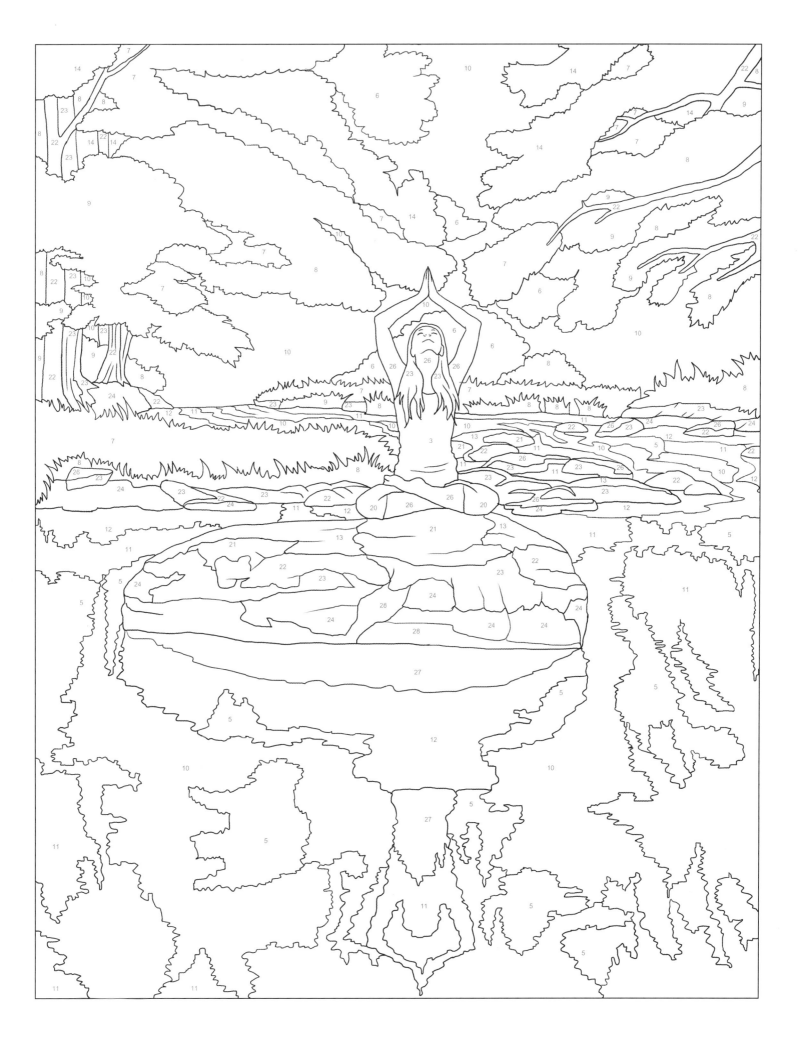

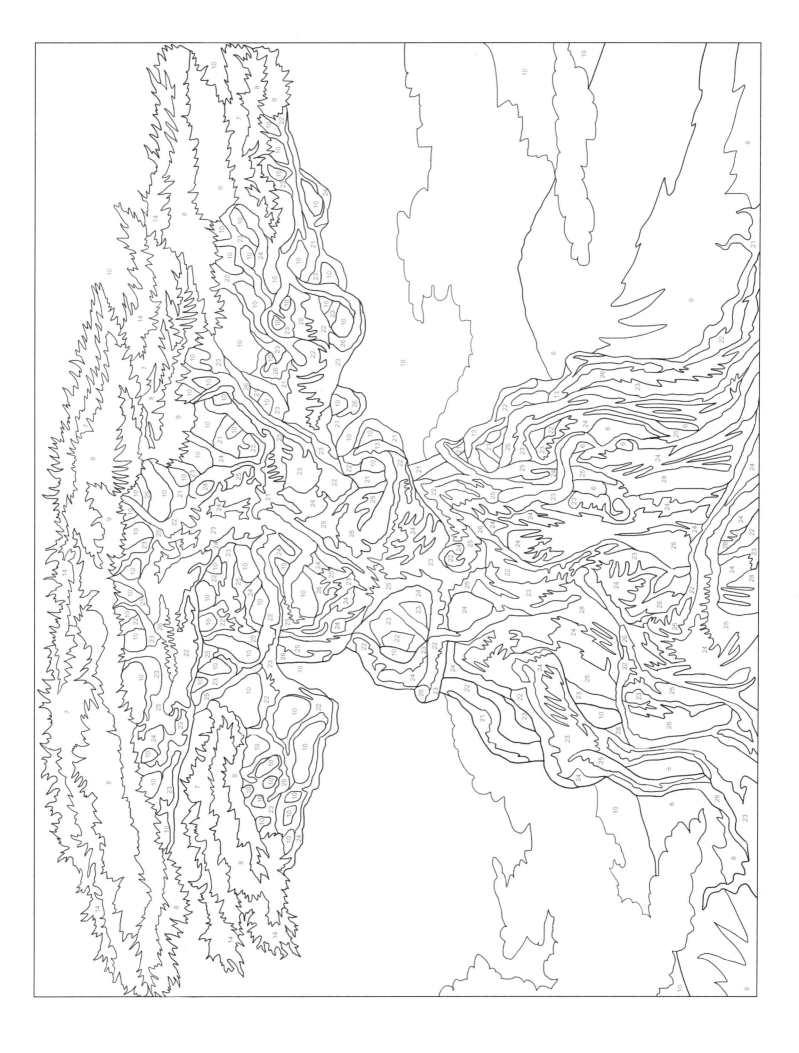

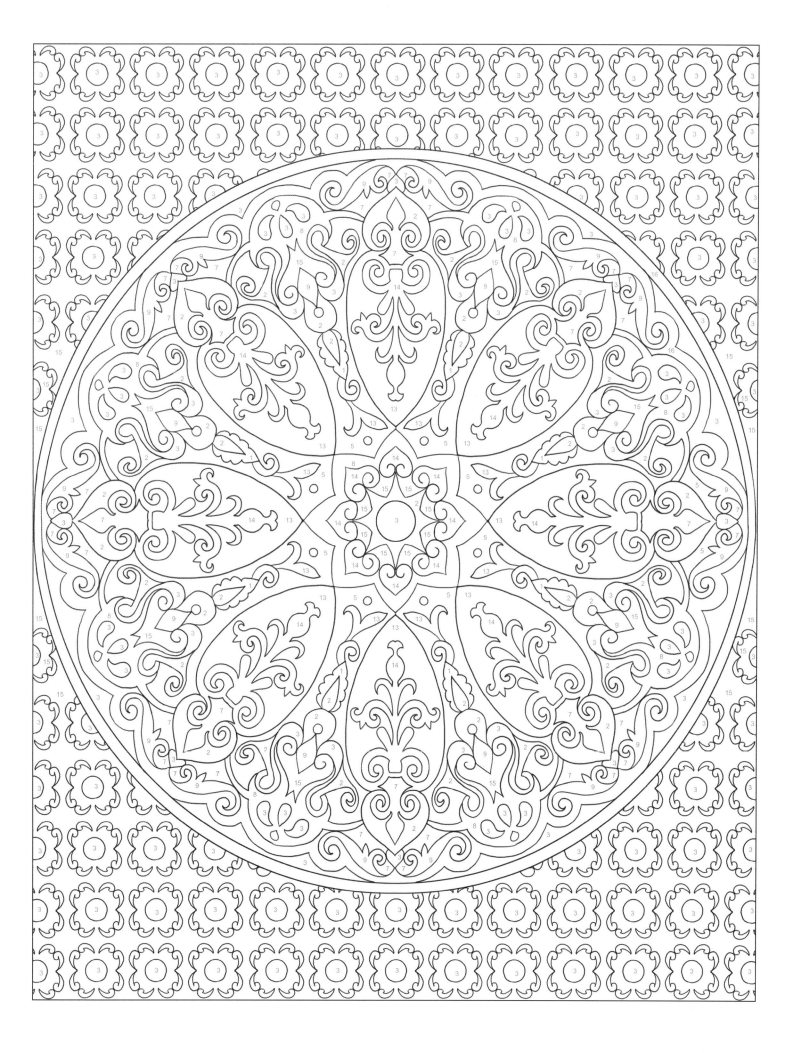

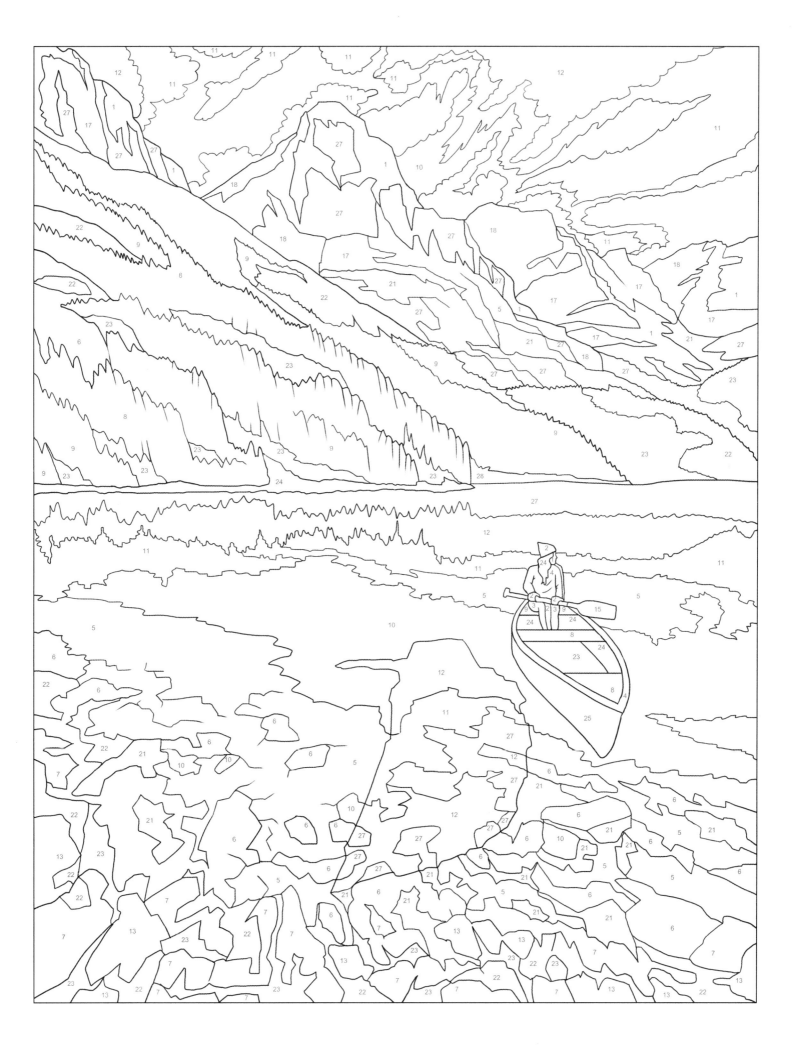

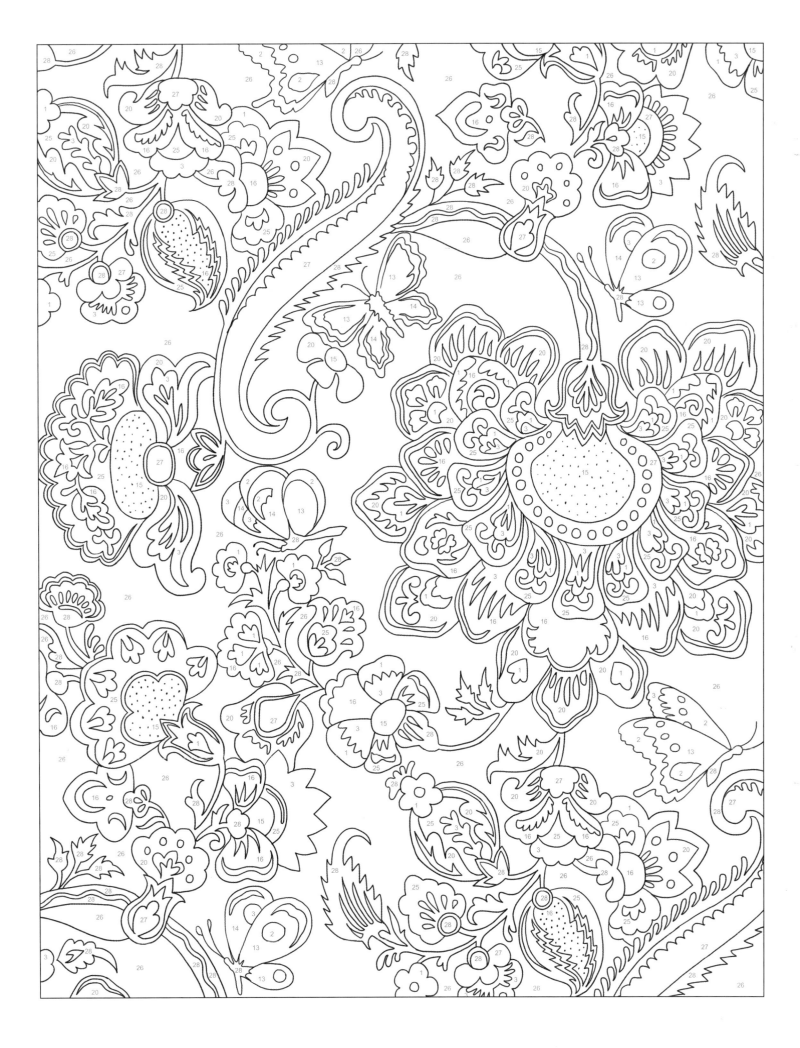

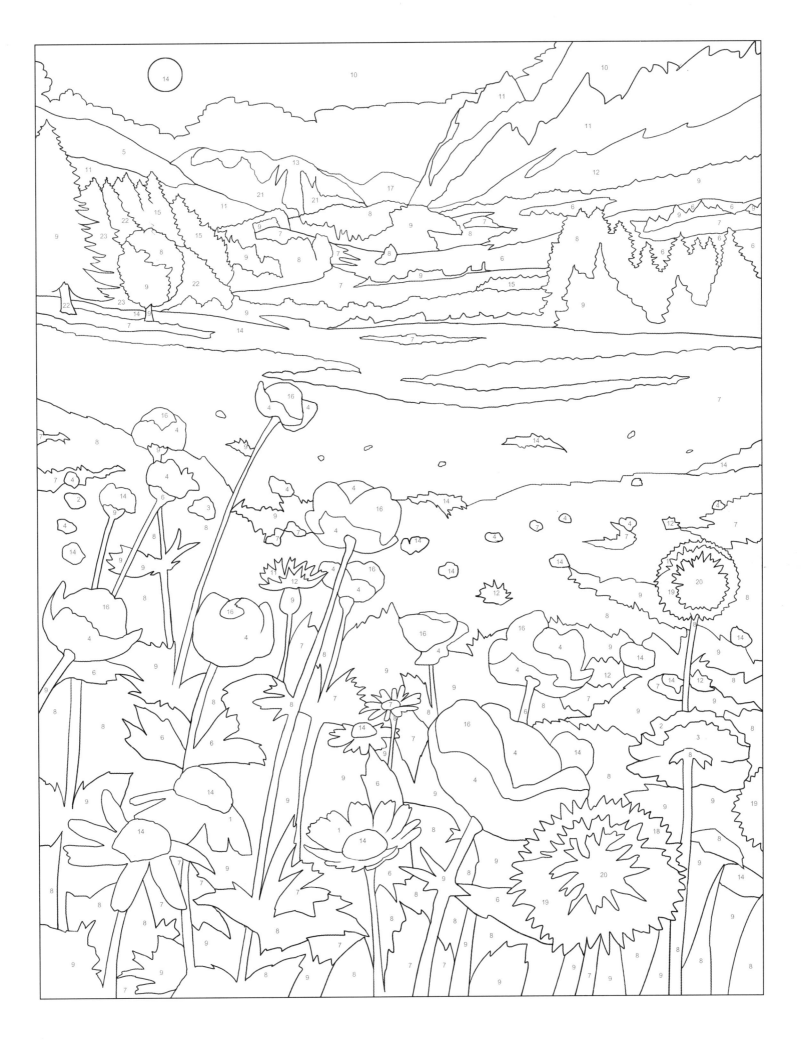

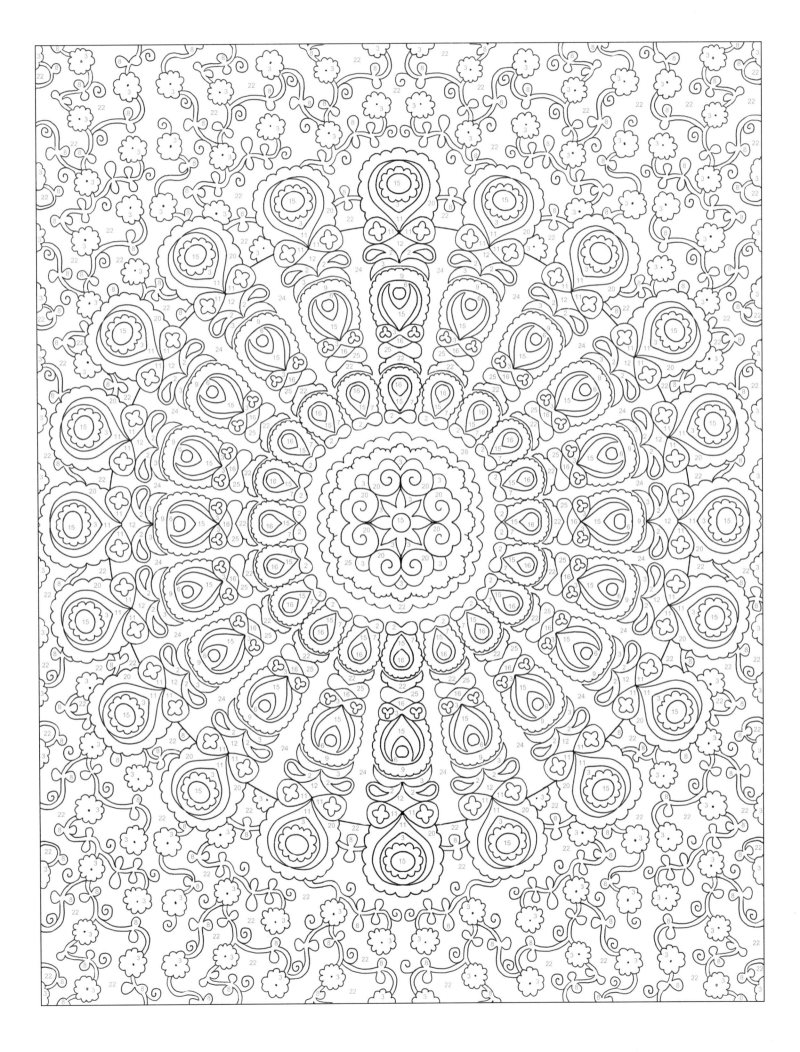

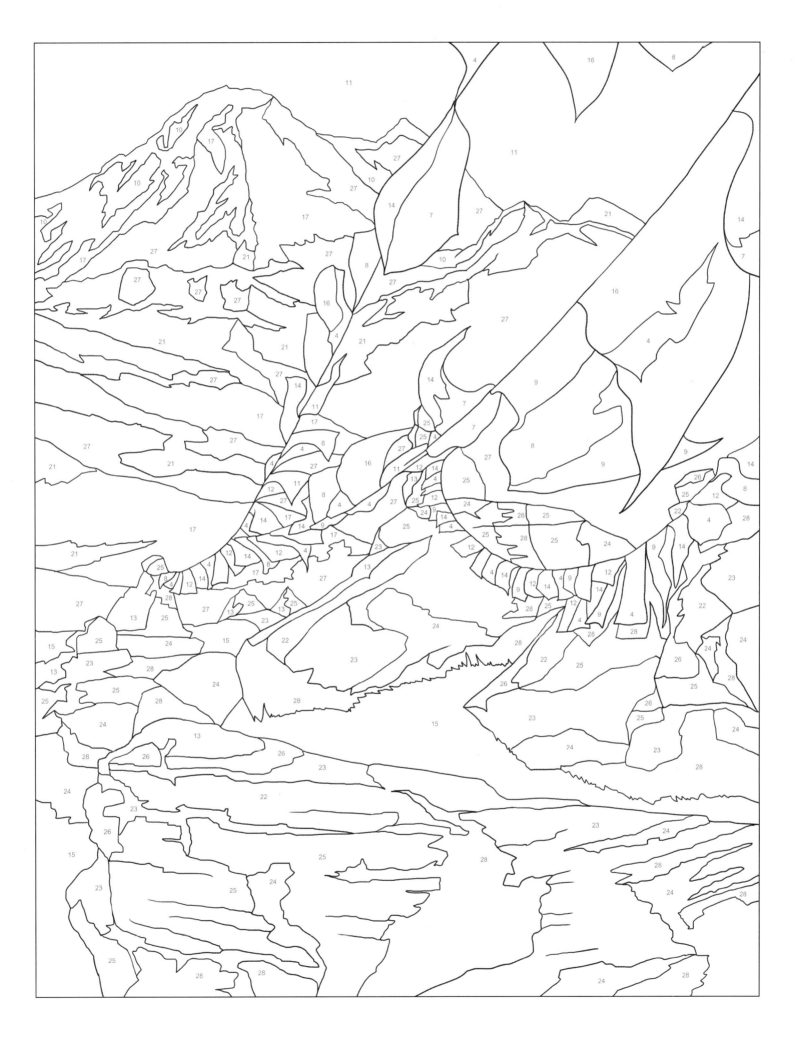

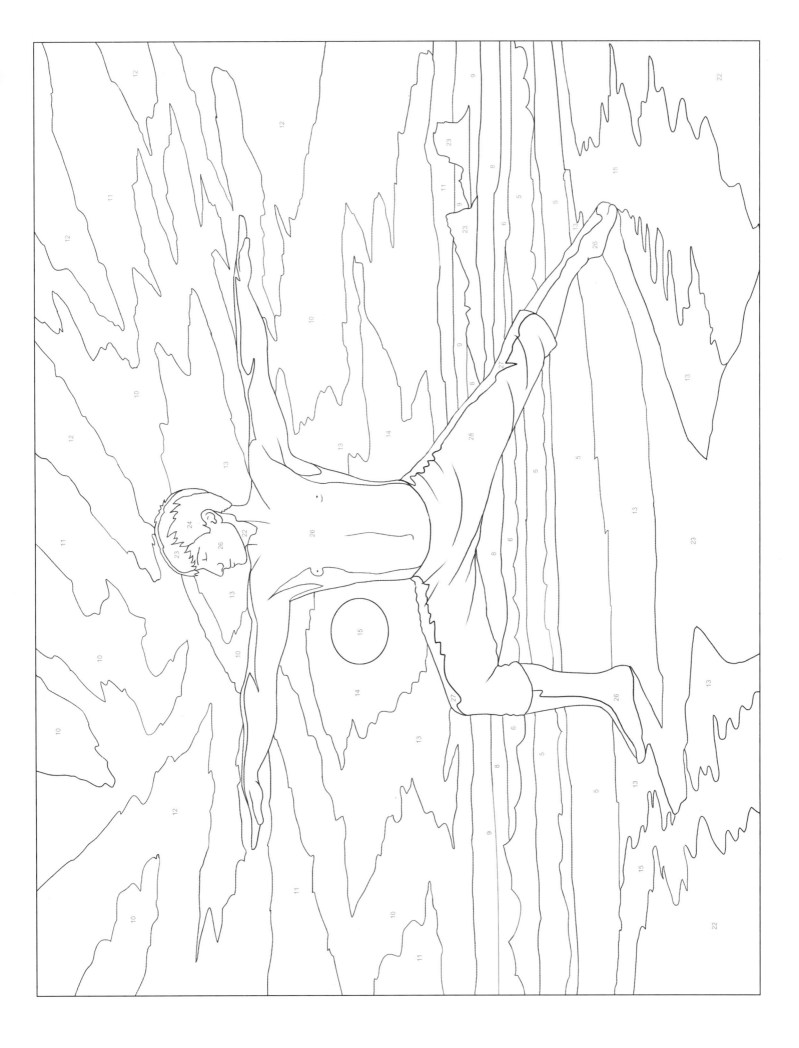

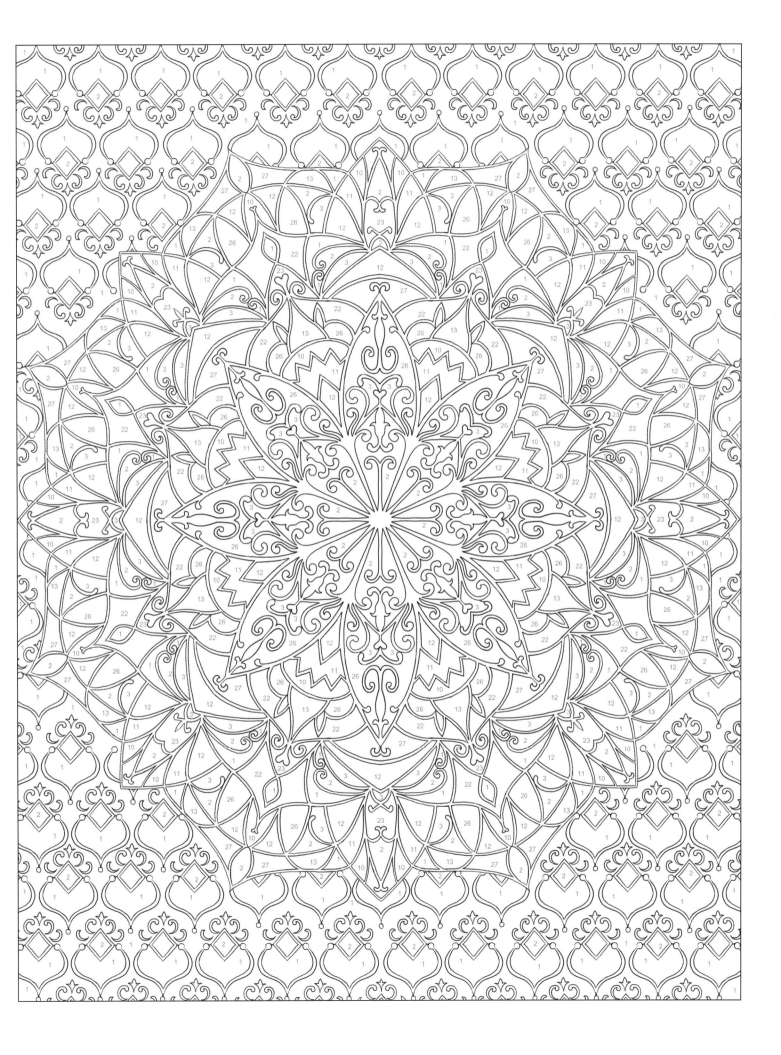

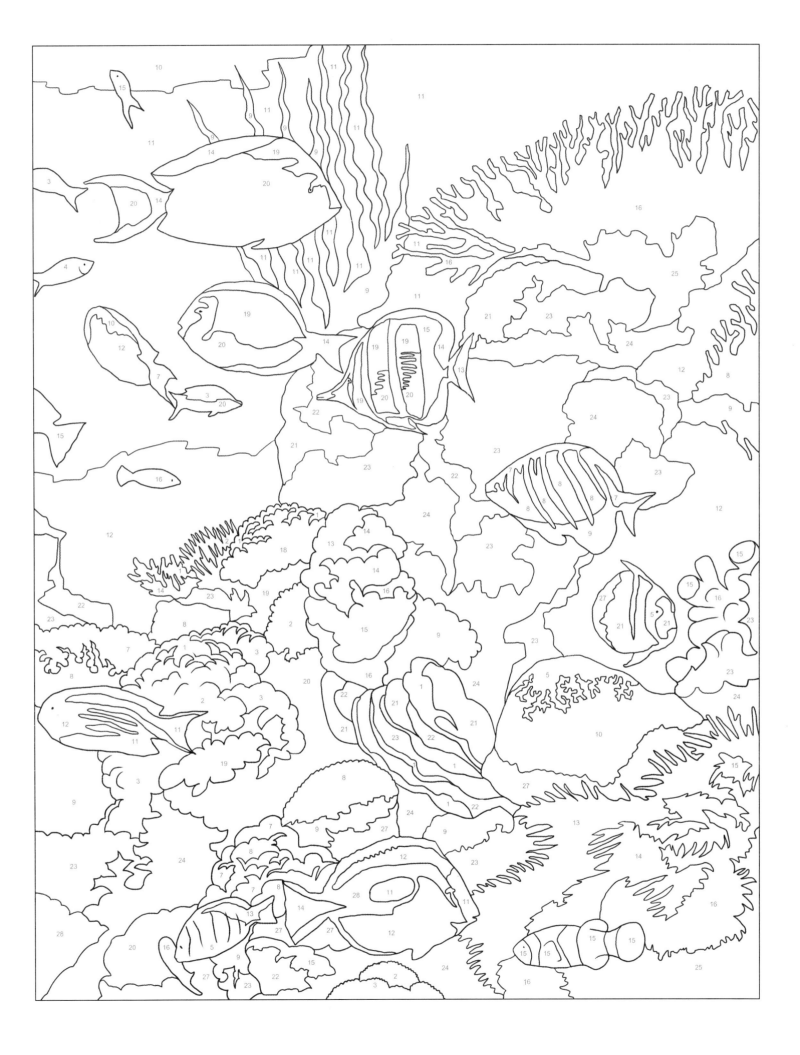

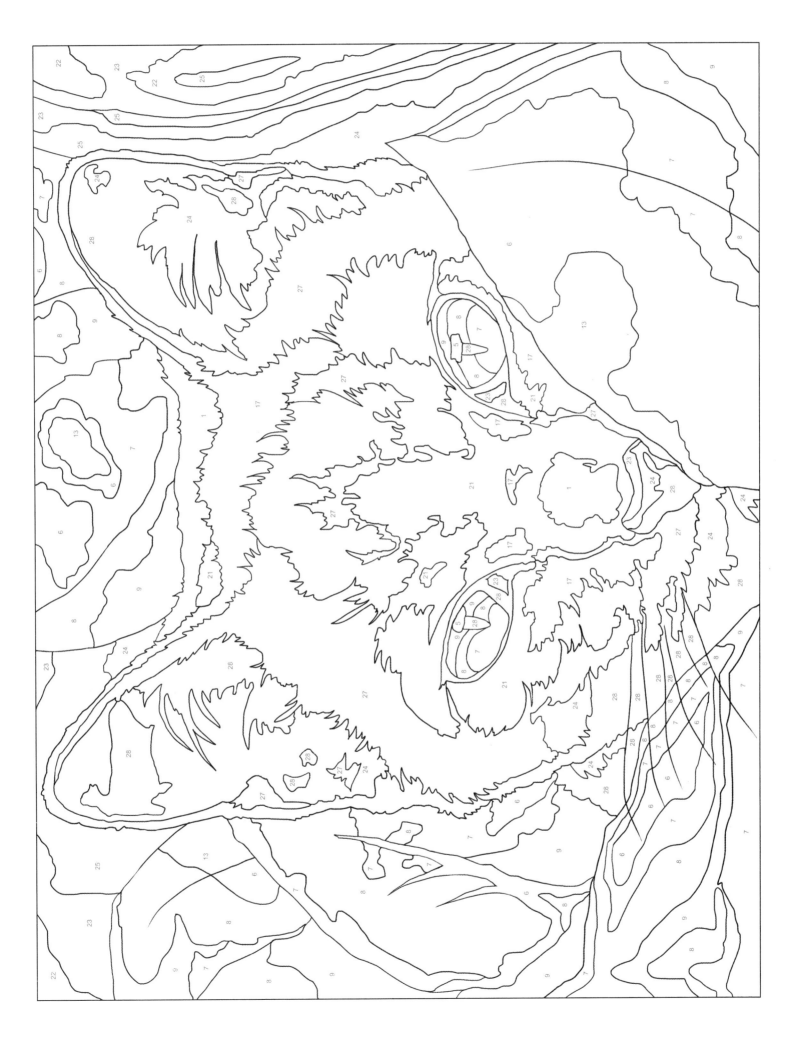

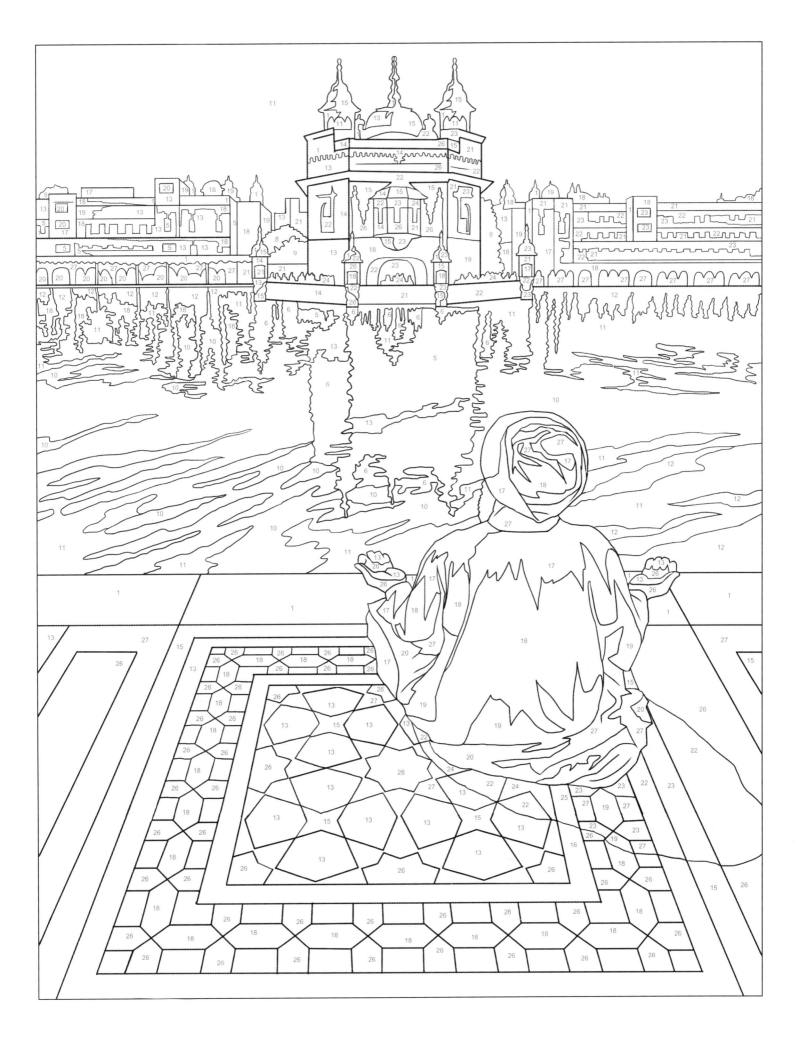

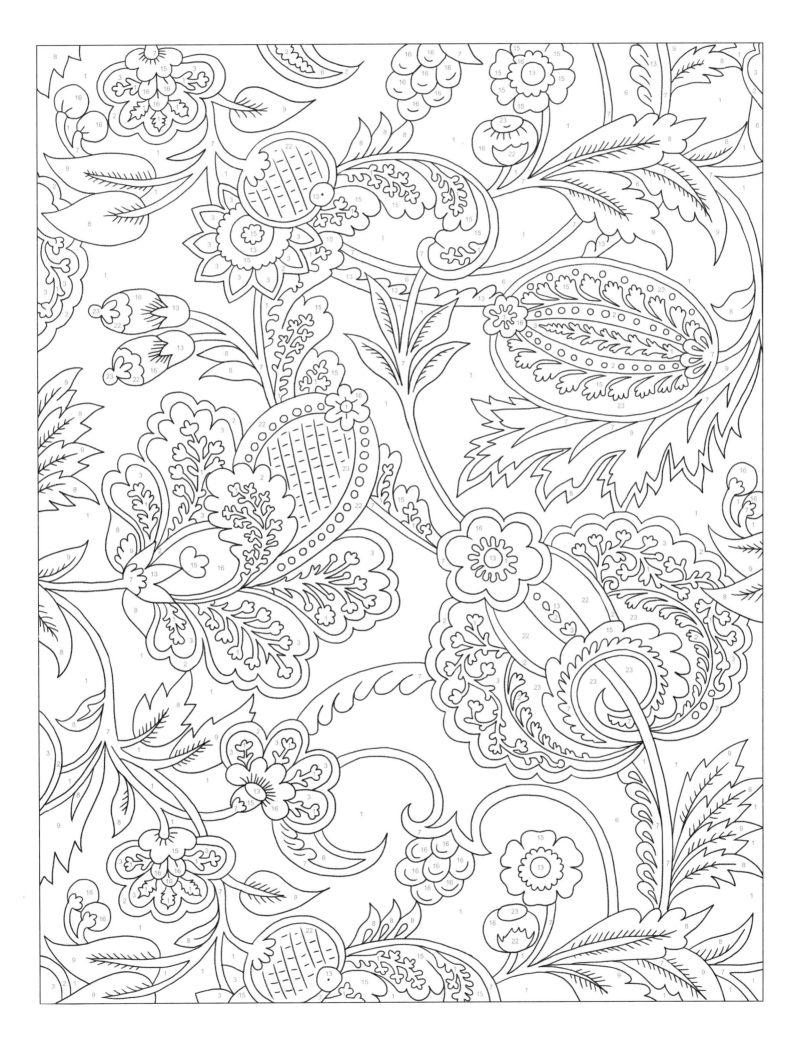

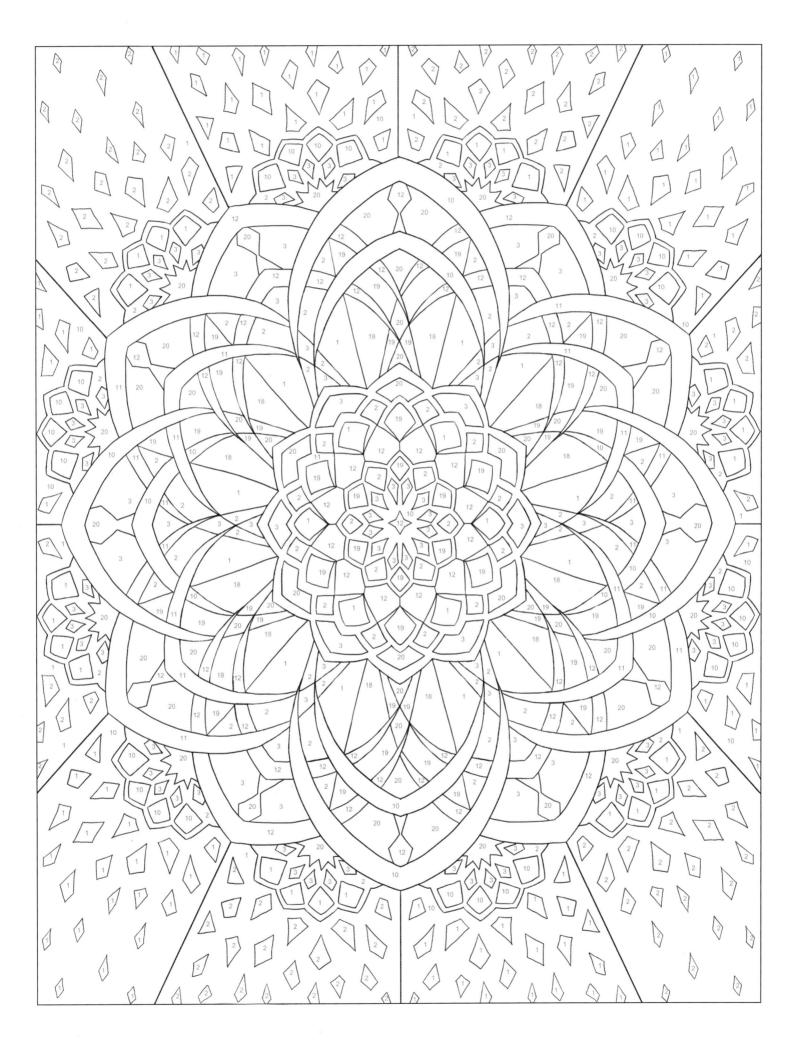

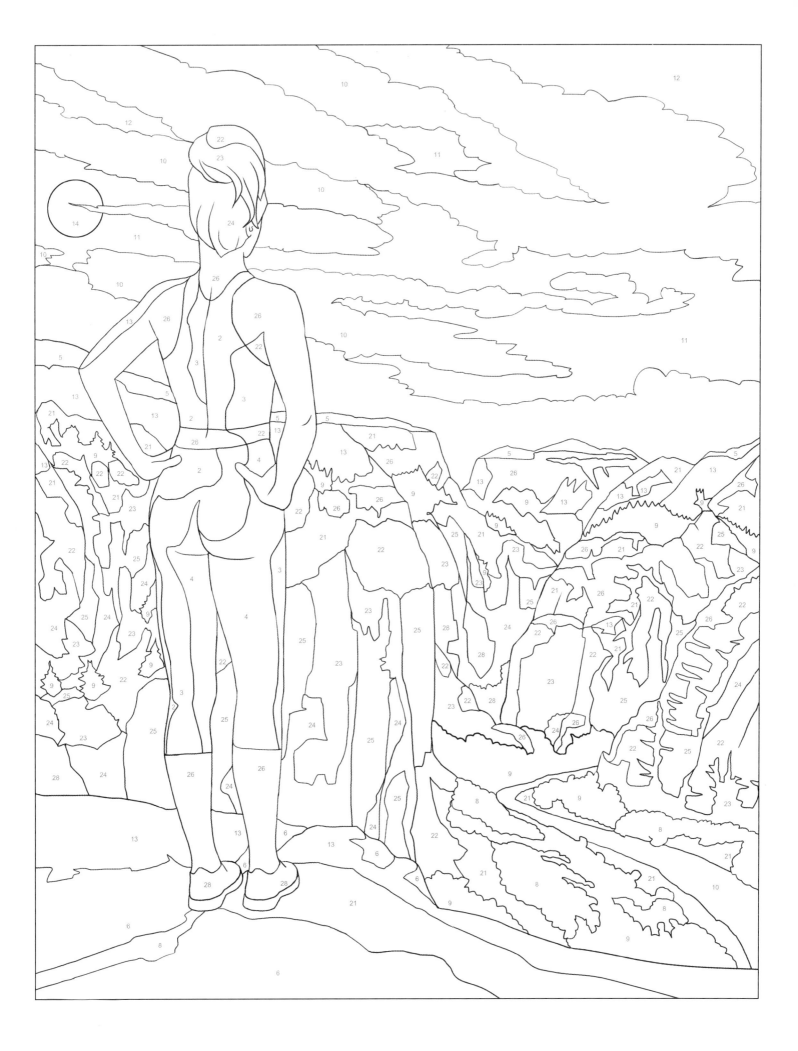

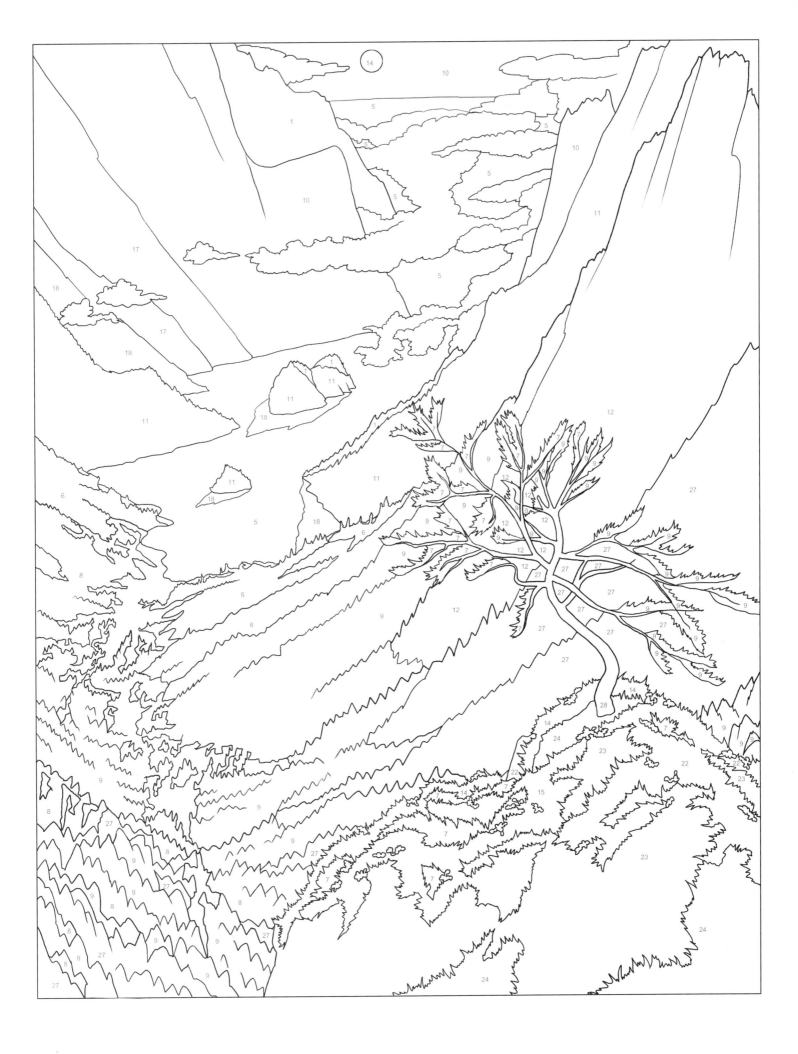

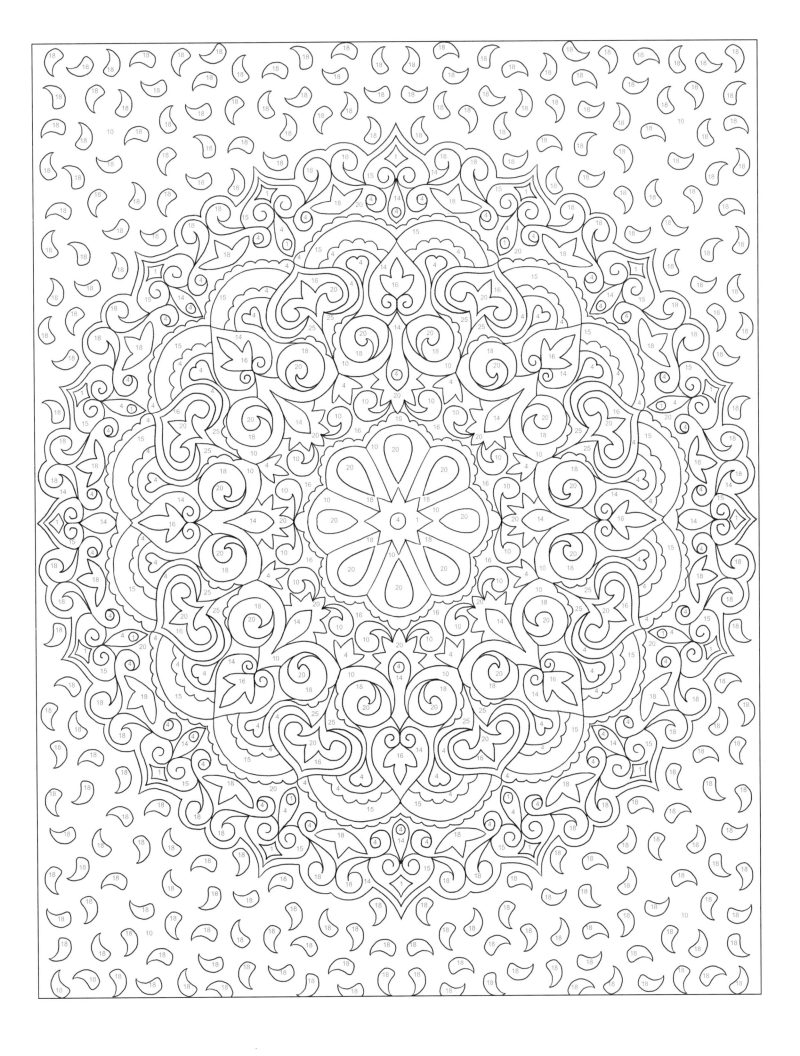

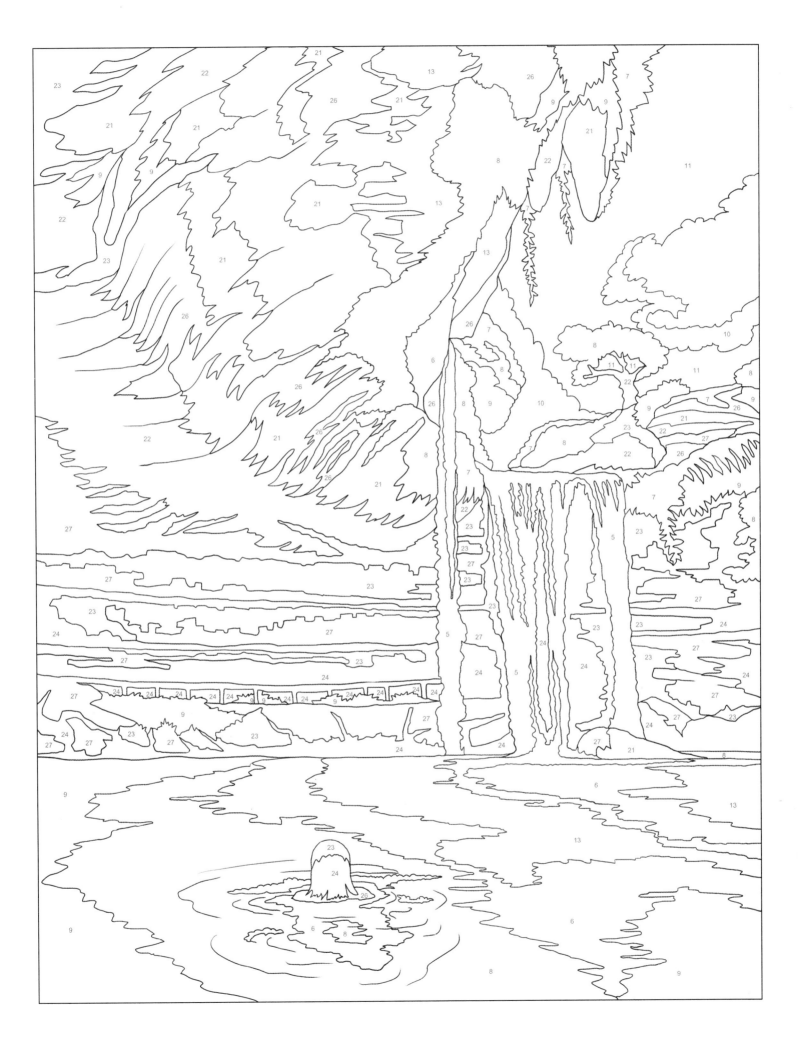

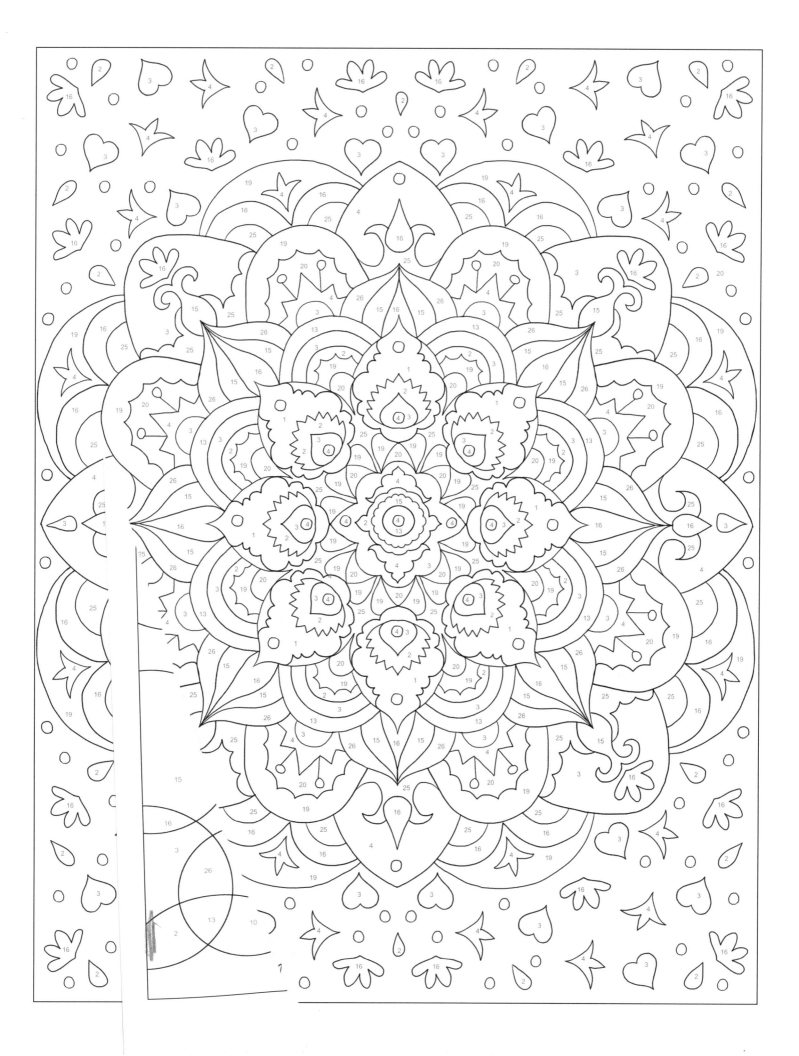

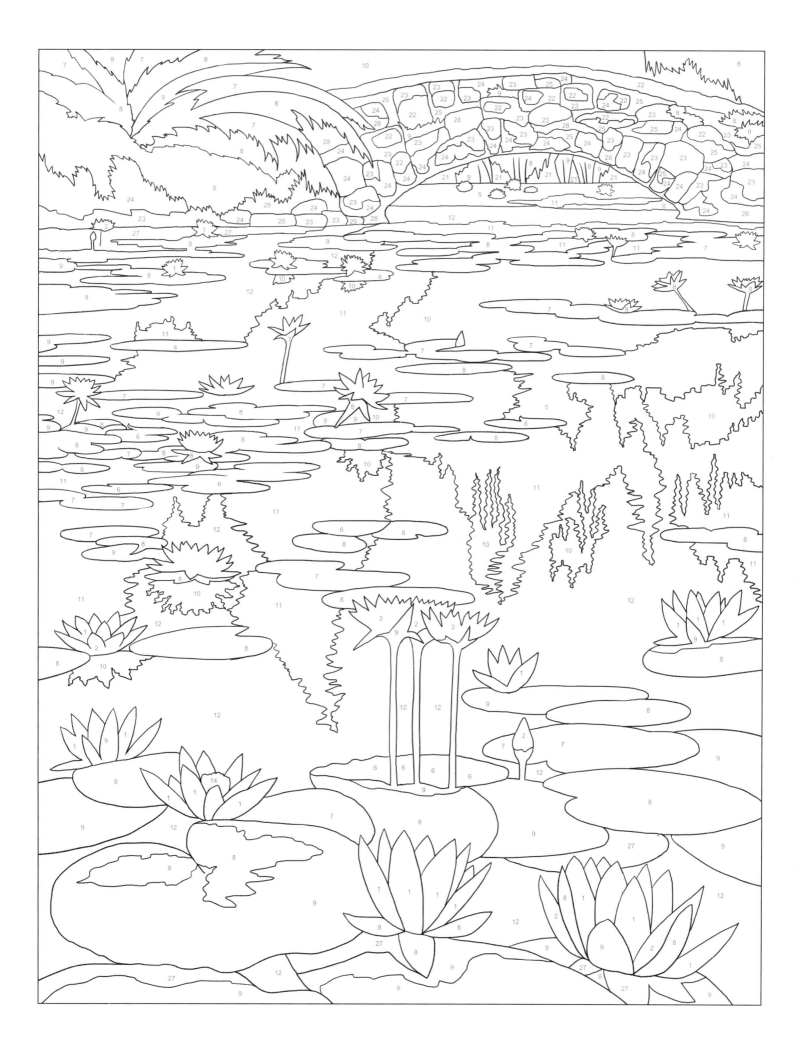

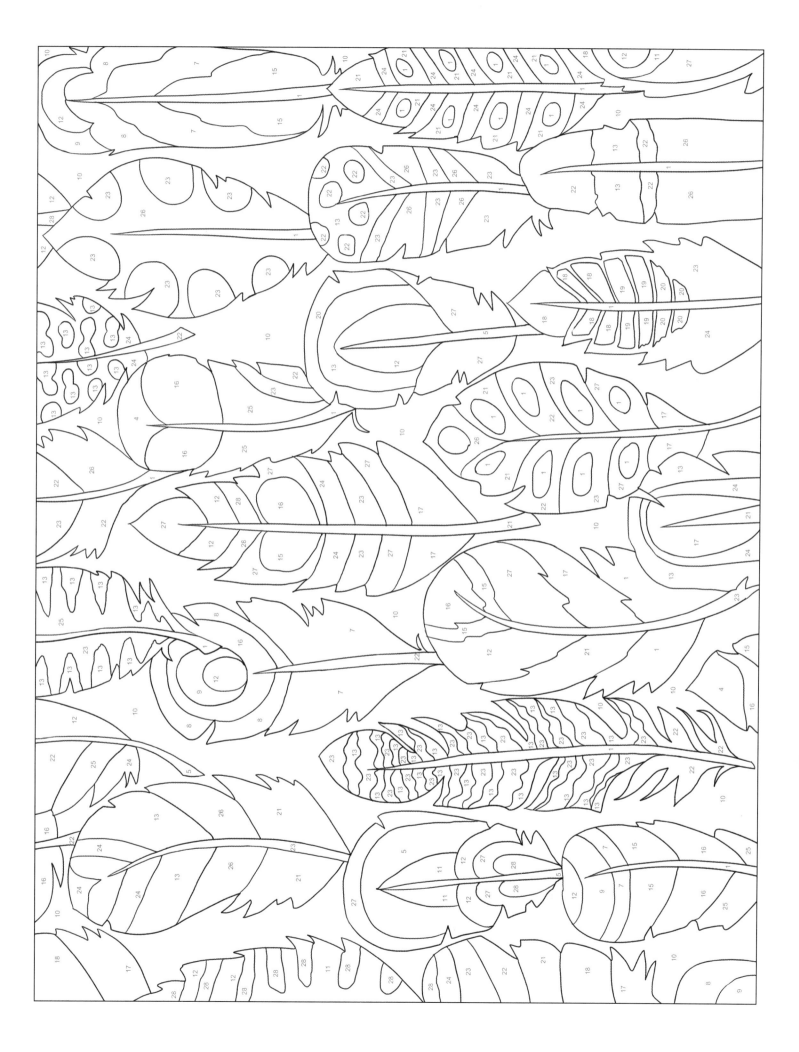